LS13

LS13

A New Generation of Leeds Writers

edited by
Wes Brown

Ink Lines

LS13

was first published in 2013 by Ink Lines
an imprint of Valley Press
Woodend, The Crescent, Scarborough, YO11 2PW
www.valleypressuk.com/inklines

ISBN: 978-1-908853-35-6

Editorial content © Wes Brown 2013

The right of Wes Brown to be identified as the
editor of this work has been asserted in accordance with
the Copyright, Designs and Patents Act 1988

All rights reserved. No part of this publication may be
reproduced, stored in or introduced into a retrieval system,
or transmitted in any form, by any means (electronic,
mechanical, photocopying, recording or otherwise) without
prior written permission from the rights holders.

A CIP record for this book is
available from the British Library

Printed and bound in Great Britain by
Imprint Digital, Upton Pyne, Exeter

This book is sold subject to the condition that it shall not,
by way of trade or otherwise, be lent, resold, hired out,
or otherwise circulated without the publisher's prior
consent in any form of binding or cover other than that
in which it is published and without a similar condition,
including this condition, being imposed on the
subsequent purchaser.

CONTENTS

Introduction 9

Adam Lowe – Monster 13
Gareth Durasow – The Last Flat Capper 19
Gareth Durasow – Notes for Future Sonnets 30
Caleb Parkin – January 2013: A Close Call with 99942 or, Pick One Fleck... 35
Caleb Parkin – A Sea Shanty for Failed Urban Development (or, The Song of Clarence Dock) 37
Cristina Archetti – Distances 39
Richard Smyth – Deep 46
Claire Stephenson – River Girl 53
Claire Stephenson – found art 56
Claire Stephenson – Untitled 1 57
Zodwa Nyoni – Big Daddy's Politiks 58
Zodwa Nyoni – Youth Service Camps: the inside story 60
Joshua Byworth – Remkear 63
Dan Annett – [Untitled] 68
AJ Kirby – Extract from Prometheus City: A Leeds Crime Novel 77
Adam Z. Robinson – Gifted 87
Adam Z. Robinson – Connivance 89
Jenny Beech – The Gap in the Curtains 91
Lizzi Hawkins – A Garden with Birds 100
Lizzi Hawkins – Time Capsule 101
Lizzi Hawkins – Trauma 104
Lizzi Hawkins – Wife 105
Lizzi Hawkins – Winter one-night stand 106
Lizzi Hawkins – Winter-thief 108
Matthew Hedley Stoppard – Leather Was Thrown 110
Sarah Brooks – Instructions in Italian 121
Sarah Brooks – Santa Trinita, Florence 123

Aissa Gallie – Film Piece: The Spaces Between Us   124
Max Dunbar – A Little Legal Difficulty   126
Matthew Bellwood – An Icy Man   143
Rosa Campbell – Antarctica   153
Rosa Campbell – Melville   155
SJ Bradley – The Life of Your Dreams   156

Contributor Biographies   161

Acknowledgements

I would like to thank a few people without whom this book would never have happened. The Leeds Big Bookend team – Fiona Gell, Liz Ward, James Loosley, David Houghton-Carter, Keith Madeley and Daniel Ingram-Brown. Mick McCann, Sammy Ingram at Waterstones Leeds, Nathan Connolly at Dead Ink, Anthony Clavane, Alison Millar at Leeds Libraries and Jamie McGarry for publishing the book in print through Valley Press.

And, finally, most importantly, the contributors and readers of this first LS Big Bookend Anthology.

Introduction

Why has there never been a Leeds book festival before? One reason might be that the Ilkley Literature Festival is on the city's doorstep and is the largest festival of its kind in the North of England. There's a strong spirit of independence among the Leeds conurbations. In recent years, Headingley LitFest, Morley Literature Festival, I Love West Leeds, Barefoot in the Park, Beeston Festival, Seacroft Literature Festival, the Leeds Independent Presses Festival. Nearby, Wakefield LitFest is up and running and the Theakston's Crime Writing Festival in Harrogate is a major festival of its kind nationally.

Leeds is alive with writing and writing-related activities. Much of it is self-organizing, located digitally or goes on in brief, wonderful bursts of energy that come and go as people come and go. Leeds is a big city. An international city. With an often fast-moving migratory population of students, workers, Leodensians.

From Transform at the West Yorkshire Playhouse, the brilliant writing being written within educational and community contexts, to the work of Peter Spafford and the EFLM team, to live literature nights like Poetry On Tap, writing groups like Leeds Savages and Fictions of Every Kind, some of my own work with Cadaverine Magazine, Dead Ink and the Young Writers' Hub. The work of Peepal Tree Press – the largest publisher of Black and Caribbean Literature in the UK – and its programme for young writers Young Inscribe. Things are happening here – no more typified than Leeds Young Author's successes at the Brave New Voices slam in Washington DC – and the award-winning documentary made about their journey to the USA.

The Leeds Big Bookend is a centrally-based Leeds festival run by volunteers. It has links, among others, with Waterstones, Leeds Library, Leeds Central Library, Leeds

Church Institute, Trinity Shopping Centre and the West Yorkshire Playhouse.

Its ambition has been to help promote Leeds-based writers, theatre-makers, storytellers, novelists, poets and readers established and new. The twenty writers we have found are by no means the definitive selection of a co-ordinated 'Leedsness'. It is intended as a snapshot of twenty writers at work or living in the city today.

Of the work included in this LS13 anthology: we have flash fiction, sea shanties, slipstream, science fiction, social realism, magic realism and old-fashioned realism. Concrete poetry, free verse, rhyming couplets, non-rhyming couplets and 'page' poetry. These works are striking in their difference. There's no suggestion of a 'Leeds movement' in any artistic sense. These poems, lyrics and fictions are all fiercely independent.

In Salman Rushdie's *Midnight's Children*, a doctor, Aadam is invited to examine the sick daughter of a landowner. To save her modesty, Aadam can only see through a hole that has been cut, a crude circle seven-inches in diameter in the middle of a cloth. He must imagine the rest. I hope LS13 is a kind of perforated sheet. A tantalizing glance into a Leodensian writing culture. What's beyond is ours to find.

Wes Brown,
May 2013

Adam Lowe

Monster

Tim

Monster smells of lavender and cumin. She is cold, ice cold, as she ties Carrot to the legs of the workbench. Those things are bolted into the floor, so he's not moving. And she looks rational, like she does this at breakfast every morning. Pours herself a glass of orange, the pulpy kind, and takes herself a bunch of hostages while waiting for the toast to brown.

She butters the toast with a machete.

Of course, we're not hostages.

She puts the barrel of the gun against my temple. 'Where'd you put it?'

Sweat pours down my face. I can feel it burning red. That's the blood rushing to my brain, loaded with adrenaline. Fight or flight. Except, I can't do either. All I can do is watch, and my breath comes out in pained jerks.

I tell her I don't know what she means, stuttering, like.

'Don't play games with me or I'll blow your brains out. Where is it?' Simple as. Monster never fucks about.

I look over to Carrot: his bright red hair and terrified green eyes. He's staring at the giant ring on her left hand. An official ring with some noble insignia on it. And the boy can't take his eyes off it. I guess it beats staring down the barrel of an antique Chinese pistol with dragons snarling at the muzzle, reminding him of his mortality.

Blam! To show she's serious, and that I'm taking too

much time, she's shot me in the ankle. Blown the foot off in a sudden blossom of blood so I fall over, screaming. The pain is instant, searing, but so immense it numbs my mind and I feel the world clouding over. My breathing becomes easier; black dots dance in ripples across my sight.

'Where is it? I won't ask again.'

Ahead, I tell her. In the safe in the TV. And I give it up just like that. Might as well. There's only one chance to kill this bitch, and I have to time it right. I can barely think straight with the pain, and I might yet bleed to death. Sulphurous smoke tickles my sinuses, unfurling from the end of her gun.

Then she squats in front of me, the sight of her filling my view. She is a mess. It's no secret why they call her Monster. She has no breasts, only two slight cavities where her vest falls against her ribs. Curved scars can be seen tracing where her mammaries should be. Gruesome burns cover her face and bald patches dot her mousy hair. She is a creature of the wastes; a sewer crocodile with patchwork skin.

'Show me,' she says, cutting me loose from the chair.

I almost faint as she plucks me out of my seat and forces me to stand on a foot and a stump. Trailing nerves and cracked bone meet cold concrete and I scream. I almost fall, but she grabs me, and I almost thank her — almost forget she did this to me.

'Move.' She prods the gun against my spine.

But this is my opportunity. I totter over to the TV, one step at a time. Black blotches flicker before my eyes and I fight against tears I can't control. Each step is laboured, delivered with a grunt and a whimper.

When I reach the TV set, I lean against it, gaining support for my lopsided frame. Taking deep breaths, I reach for the dial. I can barely see the numbers as I enter the combination, but the gun at the nape of my neck has become a white hot presence. So I have to.

'Tim...' Carrot says, panicking. 'She's going to kill us.' From the smell and the stain spreading over his trousers, I know he's emptied his bladder.

I tell him to shut up; that I need to concentrate. Yes, I need to concentrate.

The TV screen swings forward, the safe yawning with a gasp like I've opened the Ark of the Covenant. Its innards should glow, but there's only shadow in there and I'm no Harrison Ford. Suddenly smiling, Here's my chance. Do it now. Do it right.

I reach inside.

Fifty quid extra every round, I explain, showing him the dark gloss of the 9mm. It's a fine gun, polished to perfection. Guns like this, it's a shame to use them. I worry I might spoil its new gleam. A gun is never the same once it's fired: a gunpowder hymen is broken and it becomes evil. Its innocence is taken and there can be no doubt what it stands for. It's that same dark energy released when Cain killed Abel. Black powder marks the murderer for all who find him.

Carrot has never played like this before. He's an unfired pistol, too. There's something inside him, waiting to spark. Some would call it a brain. I've seen no evidence of that, so this is all supposition.

Someone just needs to pull the trigger.

Whoever backs out, I say, pays up. And this makes him nervous. Those shifty hands wring the sweat from each other. Fear draws into his cheeks.

'I've never played this before.'

This is unnecessary conversation: a tactic to delay the inevitable. But tonight I'm going to push his petty criminal mind. All little boys need to grow up.

I spin the chambers. Carrot necks one of the twelve shots lined up on the workbench. For courage of the Dutch variety. If it weren't for his skin, I reckon his skeleton would shake itself apart.

Who should go first? I ask.

He hesitates, considering the odds. Six chambers. One bullet. Two men. The numbers hung there, in the air, between us. A secret code.

'I will,' he says, downing another vodka. Russian for Russian.

With sweaty palms he takes the gun from me, an almost imperceptible tremor in his fingers.

The boy's chicken, I know, but how else will he get the guts to work for me? Khan is my biggest client at the moment, and he demands the most of my efforts. He also pays far more than any of the other crooks in the city. Best to deliver a world-class service.

Barbara Castleford, former nun and super-sharp hitwoman, was my mentor. The woman who killed JFK and Kurt Cobain and then, in her eighties, taught me all she could with a gun. Barbara: the woman who could kill anyone and get away unnoticed. See, I had to be that good. Less and I'd get caught. Get dead and get there quickly. I couldn't afford to have Carrot dithering and perspiring through a heist or a shoot out. We had to be clean, crisp.

So Carrot's levelling the gun with his stubbly sideburns and closing eyes. Praying to any god that'll hear him. I smirk and wonder how many he knows. The gods have been good to me. The bullet-proof man.

Chances: 5-1.

Click. And somebody up there's listened.

4-1. I like those odds. It's my turn, so I square the gun with my jaw, aimed upwards. One bullet would cut straight through my parietal lobe and pulp my greymatter. Bye-bye, Tim. But I don't sweat it. I always win this game.

Click. My heart's hardly quickened. You wouldn't know I've nearly died. Just a quick tour of Hell. 3-1.

Carrot's breathing heavily. I wink at him, raise a shot glass to toast my survival. He just blinks at me as fermented potato juice greases my insides in liquid fire.

He cautiously takes the pistol, as if in ritual obedience to Chaos. Again he points it at his head. Warm metal kiss to the skin. Whiff of friction. This gun an explosive whore now; her lethal capacity rendered explicit.

I can see the tendons tighten all through his arm, in his shoulder, rippling up from his fingers, which gradually, slowly, suppresses the trigger. 2-1.

Take another shot, I think. Of course, I do. Then I pick up the gun, fast-draw style, and — Click. 1-1.

Carrot takes the gun as if it will blister his hand. As if it is the plague. He knows his chances.

He flinches. He spins the chambers in defeat. 'How much do I owe you?'

The kid carries unmarked bills in a Spiderman wallet. Perhaps he's not as useless as he appears. He must've earned that money somehow. He certainly wasn't a rich kid by birth.

I tell him to put the gun in the safe as I count my winnings twice over. During the second count I hear a banging at the door. It's one of those reinforced ones, so not just anyone can break into the warehouse. With an unexpected blast, the door is in fiery pieces. She walks through, Monster, with a grenade between her teeth and a pistol in her hands.

I spin round, hoping to take her off-guard. She has her shooter in my face and I have mine in hers. Still she's cool, steady.

'Planning to use that?' she asks.

Bitch! Fucking smart-arsed bitch!

I can't answer her — just hold the gun as straight as I can and remember to breathe. 'Let's play a little game.' She's right there in my head. Prodding the fear-centre with her finger. Feels like she is.

'I hear it's a game you're good at.'

'Excellent, in fact.' I'm doing better than I expected. Blinding pain searing through my foot. Guts coiling themselves tight as serpents inside. And she's right: I'm brilliant at this game. It's called cat and mouse. It's called chess. It's called war and the rulebook was written by Sun Tzu. All I need to do is keep my mind trained on killing her and not clouded with Monster's mind games. Forget Carrot. He can fucking rot. I've got myself to think about.

'Didn't you once win twelve grand from Big Red because he lost in front of the mafia?'

I nod. Flattery from Monster? Must be another mind game. I push it out of my head. 'We'll both put down our guns after three, and then I'll swap your gun for my spare.' She indicates her left hip with a tilt of the head. 'Then we know exactly how many bullets are left and we each get to point a gun at each other to make sure no one backs out. We take turns with the one you've got now. Keep playing until one of us is dead.'

So we swap. Easy, like. We each have a gun and I'm pointing the game's revolver to my head. I never lose.

Carrot

She's monstrous. Hurts just to look at her. But I can't move anyway; I'm tied up. So I might as well look at her. Sometimes we can't help but try to stare out the pain. As if comprehension comes from, um, witnessing and relief from comprehension.

If only, as my mother would say, life were that simple. It's not. Which is why Tim's playing games with her. I figure she's always playing games.

He's, um, smiling now. For the first time. Like he knows he's going to win. But she's smiling too. Tension like they're going to eat each other or fuck or, um, maybe just explode.

I want to explode. Or maybe crawl away. I shouldn't be here.

Tim has the gun to his head.

Click.

My man lucks out. He's smiling even more.

Monster's go. She fingers the gun like, um, a sex toy. A big, black, trembling dildo. Rubbery and heavy in her hands. She slides it in her mouth, a pro. Teasing us both. She's a car-crash porn star. I feel sick.

And I can't help but notice that ring, and I think, um, that I know what it means. Thieves always know about shiny things. Only six people in the world ever had rings like that. All of them are supposed to be dead, right? Well it looks as though ghosts can shoot.

Maybe Tim'll finish off what an explosion couldn't.

Click. And she's made it, and she's alive, and that means only one thing. Three bullets for Tim.

One bullet each for me and her. That makes five.

You do know why they call it a six-shooter, right?

Tim's a trooper. He never loses. He's got something up his sleeve. Always has. Best and worst thing about him. You never know what he's gonna pull on you next.

I'm shivering now. The panic's settling back in. If he can't get out of this one, she's gonna kill me too. Coldblooded killer, she is. Killed thirteen guys in that bank robbery, um, last week. Proper vigilante bitch.

Catwoman with third degree burns.

Snot drips from Tim's nose. He's not smiling any more. Neither's she. The game's deadly serious. Holding the spare gun Monster gave him with just two fingers, he's, um, reaching behind his back. Like he's gonna reach for something with the other three fingers.

Catwoman's got her gun still locked on him. Deadly serious. Maybe even reluctant. A moment of doubt, I wonder? — but no. She nods at him. Do it, she's telling him. They both know what should be done.

Tim's fingers fiddle with his belt, nervously. There's, um, nothing there.

I shit myself the same second the gun goes off. Can't help it. Thieves deal with knives, not guns. I just let go and I'm suddenly out of it. Feels as though I'm watching it from above. Monster creases her brow, frowns a little. Then she, um, turns to me. I'm dead meat.

Smoked dodo.

But she just winks. Smiles at me and winks, then marches to the door, the shape of the key in her pocket, and walks out, right, into broad daylight. Fucking cool as Elvis.

Ides

I'm dressed in a funeral veil. That way, people can't see my face. Not that it stops them staring anyway.

The high street's dead on a late weekday afternoon. Deader than normal for this economic situation. Even during a war, people will shop. So there are only small handfuls of people, but that's enough. An orange VW Beetle is parked on the other side of the road. The girl in the backseat is watching me. She wears blue-tinted sunglasses and has neon pink hair. She's kind of hard to miss.

When she realises I've clocked her, she lifts a comic to hide her face and beckons for the driver to move on.

I can't make out the cover of the comic.

Miscreation's Celebrations is a portable stall parked up about halfway down the street, outside the pharmacy. I smile at the vendor, who is sitting behind the wooden counter in his wheelchair.

'Hey, Mack.'

He nods at me. He calls me Mary but he suspects it's not my real name. Because he never questions it, I pretend to believe he's a veteran. I read the real story in the papers: it was a high- speed collision with a police car.

'Not bad weather today,' he says.

'Better than yesterday, at least.'

Clouds melt into a pale sky above. There's sunshine, but not so you'd notice.

'What can I help you with today?'

'Can I just get the usual,' I say, awkwardly.

'Is your mother still sick?' he says with a wink.

Normally I'd make a joke, but today I'm too tired. My skin feels tight and dry; I have little patience.

As Mack inflates my three lilac balloons and wraps a bunch of marigolds in silver paper, I take a seat on the stool he keeps in front of the counter.

'What's his story?' I ask, nodding to a man in a suit and trainers jogging past.

'He's an architect. But secretly he wants to be a P.I. He reads Agatha Christie by night and smokes French cigars. Then he watches his wife and jots it all down.

'She makes long, hushed phone calls in the middle of the night. One day, he'll find the other man.'

This is the game we play.

'What about her?' he asks, pointing to a woman with a hat full of peacock feathers and a long mink coat.

'Disillusioned animal rights activist.'

'What?' He laughs.

'Her fiancé crossed the line and became a terrorist. When he was arrested, she had to move town. Her parents are filthy rich but were going to disown her. She's now making a point of buying extravagantly cruel and expensive clothes, and any cream that's been tested on animals.'

Mack's giggling like a drunken schoolgirl. A sudden

breeze lifts my veil, only momentarily, and the atmosphere peels open, a torn scab. Not wanting to upset me, Mack pretends he hasn't seen, but now I feel raw.

'So is it another busy day for you, Mary?'

Smiling as best I can: 'Yes. That's the wonder of being self-employed.'

'Aye, well make sure you take a good holiday soon!' he says as I stand and pay for my items. He smiles warmly and I accidentally bow, unsure how else to respond to this flash of camaraderie.

'Thank you,' I say. I leave quickly.

Sarah lives in a tumbledown house in a failing estate. Once, she was seen as above this. Now it doesn't matter. Bricks are bricks and hearts are hearts.

Gates are also gates, and frequently noisy, so I act the cat burglar and climb over this one. There are thirty-nine steps to her door. One for every lashing to the cross and one for every year of my life. It takes me no time at all to steal towards the window, crouching. Inside, Sarah is seated by an old gas fire. The TV bellows, garbled in the corner.

I begin to feel sick. I withdraw from the window and hurry back to the gate. There I tie the balloons and flowers.

I always run away after this. I tell myself I'm busy.

I live in shadows. I prefer it that way. A single, fading bulb offers what light there is. In the mirror I can hardly see myself. It's as if I'm a haunting; bits of me have faded away.

I remove my veil. Green eyes are revealed, almost forgotten again. My opponents reason they should be red. Then I could be the Terminator, or Carmilla, or Sonja Blue.

Sylphs have spirited my face away. Fire elementals have chewed at the bone beneath. It's all out of shape: warped like the abused wooden chair in the corner. I should pad my cheeks out with pin cushions and cover my scars with concrete. If I jerry-rigged a half inflated football in my brassiere, I could maybe call myself a woman again.

Where the light falls there are reflected whispers of flesh. In time, if I will it, the body will fall silent and the darkness will be still. For now, though, I am this little voice, and when I need to I can roar.

Monster

Neon letters shimmer across the tarmac, spelling out 'The Darkroom' upside down. The bouncers at the door recognise me and step aside. As I turn to one then the other, they stare ahead insistently. They don't want to make eye contact.

I walk inside, a sudden rush of warm, stale air meeting me. To my left are the stairs, closed off by a chain with a 'STAFF ONLY' sign hanging from it. I crouch down beneath the chain and ascend. The music fades away as I climb; there are no speakers here. At the top of the stairs is a door, its red paint flaking away from porous wood.

'Come in,' says the voice inside, and I do.

Inside the room cigar smoke swirls beneath the ceiling. Jonas Thuggee, a tall Indian man with dreadlocks, sits at a desk piled high with paper and temporary ashtrays. Cups, CD cases and shot glasses all filled with cigar dumps. On display are various hunting trophies, including the heads of a rhino, a lion and a stag.

'Hello,' he says, swivelling round to put his cigar out on the window sill. 'Bloody Mary?' I don't answer. I just take a seat across the desk from him.

'Business is slow at the moment,' he says. 'The economic downturn's all because of some war none of us wanted. It's almost enough to make a reformed man return to a life of crime.'

'I don't have time to chat about your criminal nostalgia.'

'Blunt,' he says, finishing my drink and placing the tomato juice back into the mini fridge beside his desk. 'What do you want to discuss, Ides?'

'Don't call me that,' I say with a wince.

'I'm sorry, ma'am. I forget formalities when you come storming into my office and demand to get straight to business. Your directness is catching.'

'How do I get to Khan?' I interrupt.

He looks at me from across the desk, tracing his fingers round the rim of an ash-filled mug. I sip the Bloody Mary, careful not to break my eye contact with him. Fear is his province, terror his crown. He's a Brahmin of intimidation. Legendary back in the day.

'How appropriate right?' And I know he means the drink. 'A Bloody Mary for a gore-stained angel such as yourself.' Sarcasm comes naturally to him. It oozes from his lips. It's all about game for him. Thuggee loves new prey. But with me, he knows he's met another predator. Instead, he likes to play. He toys with me, waiting to see if I strike.

'How do I find him?'

Thuggee looks at me, his dreadlocks resting like tentacles at his shoulders and his aquiline nose raised slightly.

'Why do you want to know?'

'He's holding the fucking city to ransom,' I say, steady.

'You think he'll call our bluff?'

I nod. There's no way Khan doesn't mean business. I've met him before, or at least his lackeys.

Thuggee crosses his brown hands and smiles. 'I'll give you all the information you need.' 'What's the catch?' I say, because there always is one.

'Bring me...' He seems to mull this over. 'The head of the Beowulf.'

'The Beowulf?'

He nods. He probably wants to mount the fucker and say

he killed it with his own hands. It's then I wonder how many of these beasts he's actually hunted himself.

I extend my hand and he takes it. We shake and then I know it's time for another kill.

Nowell

First I see her steamy breath and then she enters like doom. A sudden chill crisps the air; I imagine I can feel the pages in my book crumble. Silvery scars glimmer in the library lights. Half her top lip is gone, so I can see her perfect teeth. Hollywood actresses kill for teeth like that. She could be Doris Day's stunt double if Doris played Freddie Krueger.

There's something of a glide about her movement. Something of the surgeon's knife sliding through skin and muscle. Easy and precise. She cuts toward me, sits down. That nonchalance in her eyes. Does it ever die?

'Dr Codex,' she says with a simple nod.

'Ma'am,' I reply.

'I need your advice.'

What else could anyone need me for?

'Advice? Certainly. Advice I can give in abundance.' I smile. I've seen worse faces in my time, but not many. Once upon a time she was beautiful.

'Tell me about the Beowulf, Dr Codex.'

'Please. Call me Nowell.' This I offer her out of respect. I was a great scientist once. Now I am nothing but an exile. We have that in common.

'Nowell,' she says, feeling her way around the word.

Then I slam my book closed, my enthusiasm waxing.

'The Beowulf...' I pause. I want to make sure I have a captive audience. But there's no need with Monster: there are so many holes about her persona she can't help but absorb. In the artificial light I can almost see through her skin.

I begin again:

'The Beowulf was created during the Second Gulf War. It was a product of the fascist revolutionaries before they came to power. It was ... he was the son of the Northern Army's then leader, General Griffiths. He was supposed to be the Neitzschean superman.'

She grits her teeth. 'How do I kill it?'

'I tried myself. Back in my bounty-hunter days. I've got a cybernetic spine to show for it.' She's not scared. Or if she is, she knows how to hide it. I guess the fear melted away with her face.

'There's only one way...'

'Isn't there always?'

'Under its ribs. At the solar plexus.'

Her face splits wide. A smile, or something like it. A rent leading to Hell.

'And where is it?'

'If it's anywhere, it'll be near the river in Old Town. It likes the waters.'

And then she's gone: pulling away and fading into the night outside. She has no time for thankyous and goodbyes; she's on a mission.

Beowulf

Woman finds me. Smells of spice. Face a mess and gun in hand. Sword at her back. She gargoyle woman. She ghost with anger inside.

I taste her on my mouth. Taste her as she close. My mouth begin to water. Fooding tonight.

Monster

This beast towers above me. Its muscles are artists' nudes strewn around its body. A blond mane of hair crowns its head and freckles shift in complex patterns across its fair skin. Water drips from the rusting bridge and slithers across its sinews.

'Fooding tonight,' it says, and I can smell rot and blood on its breath.

I raise my pistol and aim for the solar plexus. This is almost too easy, which means —

The creature grabs my hand and twists the gun free. I hear the loud snap of splintering radius and ulna. Blood fills the space behind my skin, a vein ruptured within. Then it picks me up and hurls me against the wall. Old wounds weep on my back and I struggle to keep my cool. The cold steel of my blade digs into my back.

My head fizzes like a dropped cola can. Bubbles rush to the surface of my consciousness, bringing images... I remember Sarah. I remember Sarah. I remember the heat of a burning house and beating against glass to break free. I remember breathing smoke and howling into inferno roar. Looking up into darkness. Feeling the lick of fire and smelling molten flesh. I remember baptism and pain. Then I remember before that. I remember disfigurement by other means. I remember the medical report in my lap, a Dead Sea Scroll. Heresy against the body. My breasts feeling heavy and alien on my ribs. I remember the operating table, the smell of clean, the smell of knife, the smell of blood. I remember the kiss of cold metal curving along me like a lover, against my skin like ... like the blade that digs into my back. Digs into my back now. I remember Sarah.

I'm up, my heart racing against the pain. Tearing the sword from my back, I charge at the mutant. Though it attempts a punch, I dodge it with a sudden jerk to the left and bring my sword against its chest, ripping through genetically engineered flesh. But the Beowulf is fast and bats me to the tarmac, taking my sword and shattering it like so much glass against the bridge. Smell of scorch and damp gravel.

The fizzing returns in another wave, crowding my sinuses as blood issues from my face, curling over my lip, into my mouth, down my chin and onto my shirt. My foe locks its massive fists together and moves to slam them down on my spine. Spinning onto my back, I grab the hilt of the broken sword and jab upwards, slicing into the velvety tissues of its solar plexus. Flesh gives, yielding to the cut of the jagged weapon as any meat might, grown in a vat or not. I drive it deeper, cutting under the ribs and into its pulsating heart. Against my knuckles, the organ is smooth, quivering, and bursts with a sticky torrent of blood.

The beast tumbles in a splatter of gore, my clothes drenched in dark splashes. I scramble for my gun and fire three quick blasts at its throat, severing much of the head from the neck. With the broken sword I cut through the few remaining tendons attaching head to body, then lift Thuggee's trophy to examine my gruesome success. Now dead, the beast seems more human: its eyes are softer, human eyes; its mouth set in a slight frown; its hair limp, fluttering as though an advert for anti-dandruff shampoo.

For a moment I pause: a mark of respect for my fallen adversary. For all intents and purposes, he was an innocent. An animal-man without conscience, without socialising. A lab experiment turned loose and left to run wild.

But I straighten up, embolden again. This is my task. This is who I am.

GARETH DURASOW

The Last Flat Capper

The last flat cap, worn unto death by Castleford's pantheon
faces black as the seams they dreamt of
relentless beside their wives
slate grey from lives spent stoking

men in repose behind bastion walls of pint pots
embossed with their names
and ceramic ashtrays now for shelling nuts.
A grown man cried when sent to smoke in the open air

deceased in all but his John Smiths arm mechanism
his winding wheel of reminiscence.
I'll remember him after the rings have been unscrewed from his knuckles,
the roll-up filched from behind his ear, the gold tooth levered from his rictus.

GARETH DURASOW

Notes for Future Sonnets

1.

April brought a kind of madness to the country folk
thawing inside their marital cauls
dust mites fossilised in the sinus coral
eyes open like jpegs.
Emergency callout, 6am
a bumblebee slit its saccharine guts
Stylus of blood in the eye of Apollo
Dry stone walls along the girdle of Venus.
Gotta go nan, am totally pissed,
said the girl on the train, so petite she could of died
had my empty can of Rubicon
come rolling by again. To let her hold my hand
meant gambling her fingers; I wonder if she made it
all the way to Rochdale, I wonder if she made it
all the way to Christmas.

2.

When you grow up, do you want to conduct a symphony
   of steam trains
or descend like a disco ball deep into the anvil with the
   hammerheads?
To trade all this in for a misbegotten sense of gamer
   entitlement,
the strength to left-click your enemies to death
to tap your phone for an entire commute
just to keep that little man running.

Will you plant the kiss of life upon a grandmother clock
rescued from a skip, stuck mid-slap across the chops
to the numeral next in line to wash its hands of us,
to chop it down with the edge of its hand
the mountain you make out of a milk tooth.
Cloned from the muck on your dad's guitar strings,

are you preordained to audit the stuff soaking up pavement;
a glove, a glove, a leaf, a glove,
to pull your weight like the tank engine you loved
with his moon face and capacity to sneeze,
so if ever you lose an arm, no-one pities the ease
with which it's picked up off the floor and carried to triage.

3.

We affront our dads and their razor of choice. Pastors of the
    foam and most deliberate genuflection
How they regard us, their looks askance in misted mirrors
Our nails too precious, cuticles too soft to see Subbuteo
    through to injury time
Our schooling and temperament
detrimental to one's ability to work like a man
Our every muse a spanner in his ball sack.

Was ever he aroused by the blurb on a Rimbaud Collected
'...his stormy affair...', '...nomadic adventures...'
how what starts with a barber ends up in the heliotropes
sufficient to write on the woodchip intended to muffle
the clangers we drop in our washing up bowls.

Does he think to appropriate wooden dowels from the
    workplace
for the purpose of knocking them into our ear-'oles
driving home the sense to keep our most lucrative fingers
far from the teeth of his circular saw.

4.

Springtime caprices, sky the constitution of Commodore
the wind strong enough to lift an Amiga 500
and scatter floppy disks.
Between my left thumb and forefinger, your bra clasp,
O sweet entrant from country with
higher incidence of tuberculosis,

your daily labour up to press
the adherence of stickers,
slicing liver into cut price chunks,
flaming plastic, my queen of the slatwall bend
the extent of your malice a curse along the lines
'I hope your rabbit dies and you can't sell the hutch'

wishing the pianist in my phone underfoot
that the crickets inside would eat their hind legs.
My sleeping file-sharer, how ruthless you are at freeing up disk space
How you can drag and drop *A Beautiful Mind* into the recycle bin straight at the credits
and by committing this to paper I incriminate you to the likes of the Federation Against Copyright Theft.

5.

Back when I lived, I lived off the platinum hairs unearthed in my mouth
the ones that fell from the pin-up girl above my bed
Blu tack crucifiction
fit for the nose on a flying fortress
strafed across the midriff
by the brains of Willy Messerschmitt.
I chased double-yellow lines down the drain
after butterfingered coppers
invested in teapigs
at the café where Dogsbody drummed on the counter
 expecting the cutlery to show she's the fairest,
a gnat alighting, primed to complete
the double-barrelled rose tattooed behind her ear
then drunk on indelible ink by the tenth of a teaspoon,
tucked itself into the stutter of Zeus.

CALEB PARKIN

January 2013: A Close Call with 99942 or, Pick One Fleck...

...Just one, from the hole-
punched carbon sky and wonder
at its stats, its vital ballistics. Wonder
whether cosmic winds blow it
our way; whether Newton or some other
more modern, more menacing, model
may stack odds against Earth's favour.

The roulette ball: Apophis
freewheels the not-so-clockwork model
above my head. No, not above our heads:
around them, spinning like cartoon concussion,
a character impacted. The Micky Mouse
Milky-Way squeeze-and-stretches
the life-expectancy of this
billions-years-young billiard ball.

Twenty twenty-nine, the next time. Visions blurred,
screens thick with dust of fear. When
Hollywood Lears hover near
cinema seats, with light-shows projected
from our eyes and back into the dinosaur-mind.

When masses collect on mountaintops, looking up
through rehashed prisms of extra-
terrestrial life-guards and super-
natural knowledge of ancient civilisations long-
since ceased and of hyper-
sensory conspiracies of inept governments
who somehow rule the stars.

When shots are littered every second
at worlds within our own, this speck of glitter
in the eye of space could make it blink
the ground into its own reflection, infinite bits,
out of being. But how lucky we would be
to see it, to be here: when there are more dead
than living than ever. How lucky to see
the last crater-act, the final flaming curtain.
To be the ones who saw it happen.

CALEB PARKIN

A Sea Shanty for Failed Urban Development
(or, The Song of Clarence Dock)

In the Early Noughties, 'pon the booming swell,
It was BUY BUY BUY, it was SELL SELL SELL:
So they built above the water of Clarence Dock
Lots of luxury apartments and chichi shops.

Chorus:
Oh the Dock, she be in a right old mess,
With her Pizza Express and her Tesco Express
And her – yes – her Holiday-Inn Express:
They're the only things fast enough to float,
Except for curry houses and narrow boats.

And they built a special section with its own jetty
Where all the fancy floating restaurants would be:
Now the only thing a-moored around the butts of fags
Are the blue-striped plastic carrier bags.

Chorus

Sometimes in the night you can hear the hullaballoo
Of some merry-making drunks (who are only passing
   through).
But the only voices bouncing off the moored ships' hulls
Are the quacking ducks' and the screeching gulls'.

Chorus

Now in an empty window of an old high-fashion store
There's a hopeful artist's image of what could have come before.
Yes like the ocean's waves, there is one thing that you can trust:
That after there's a boom, there will always be a bust.

Repeat last two lines

CRISTINA ARCHETTI

Distances

Time was running out. And so was space.

He was still strapped to his chair, unable to move. Blood had first curdled on the footrest, where his left foot would have been. Now it was a dry compact matter the texture of a freeze-dried meal.

The main navigation lights had gone. Only few emergency leds still twinkled from the control board. They had at first flashed alarmingly at him. Now their rhythmic lighting seemed a fraction of an eyeblink slower. How could that be? Photons should have still been reaching the back of his retina, forming a reverse image of the lights' arrangement on the control board, being converted into electric impulses, transmitted to the optic nerve, and processed by his thalamus. The control lights blurred and merged with constellations light-years away at the centre of the screen. As if staring from inside a tunnel, he could no longer see the stars streaming away like falling meteors at the edge of his field of vision. He knew his body was shutting down. Would Father be disappointed?

The titanium structure around him was travelling at 4.47 astronomical units. Only five times short the speed of light. Yet in his drifting in and out of consciousness he had the illusion of complete and weightless stillness. Had he, like his Father, ever lived on Earth, he would have thought he was asleep on a boat led by hidden currents. Perhaps along one of those watercourses that before the Great Impact were called rivers. He could have convinced himself that the background noise was the sound of breeze caressing the grass along the banks. Instead, he had been cloned in vitro on the Platform. He was like an embryo surrounded by robotic feeding systems. Just like those Father had sent into deep space to continue the exploration programme. The sound he could hear was the confirmation that they had become the last opportunity for his species to survive.

At some intervals—he had no idea of what counted as long or short—a beeping noise reminded him that he was still alive. It also gave him the illusion that he was not alone on the spacepod. And this time he really was not.

'Good morning,' said a female voice whispering into his right ear. The soundwaves travelled all the way through the auditory canal and hit the eardrum. He heard words. The sudden sharpness of sound sent his pulse into acceleration. The geometry of shapes in the control room disappeared into a vortex. The cochlea in his middle ear fired off wild electric impulses to the synapses in his motor cortex. The fingers of his bionic arm twitched. He thought of the wing flutter of the giant orthoptera that were bred at the Platform.

'It is 6.00am Earth time' continued the voice. Every time he had heard the mention of Earth he had asked himself the same question. It should not have been a priority now. But the power of automatic reflex took over his brain for the last time. Why was Father so attached to a place that no longer existed? Once more he did not find an answer.

'Coordinates: Sector 7B of Perseus Spiral Arm. We will be entering sector C in 13,987.7 time units,' came the familiar announcement marking the start of a new working routine. 'How are you?' she asked, utterly indifferent to his agony.

He could still hear It behind the door. Or was the sound made by the blood throbbing inside his ears? A coarse and slightly hissing sound, like a last breath that did not want to end.

He tried to focus, struggling to collect enough air in his diaphragm to project a sound.

'I am sorry,' announced the voice with the same slight disappointment his Father showed when he did not understand something he had said. 'No input received.'

'How are you?'

His vocal chords only managed a low groan, still below the 12 sound unit detection threshold.

'Abnormal body temperature.' She spoke again in a monotone voice. 'Temperature decreasing. Check up required.'

They had been through the same exchange twice before. But she had no memory. She only collected records, pulses of electricity travelling instantaneously through fiber optic wires. Clouds of information triggering chain reactions of variable length across shorter or longer circuits, but never forming a meaningful picture. For her, EhVA, as for any other navigation assistant, there was no time. The pod was just a space of relentless measuring and detection.

He could sense this activity, as if the walls of the pod were covered in invisible formicidae. He had seen them in the Platform laboratory. His Father called them ants. They had feverishly swarmed round a glass cage to mend the formicarium the other Fathers had destroyed to examine the creatures' resilience. Exactly what his brain was trying to do right now — attempting to manage the energy reserves left and the missing parts before it was too late. His brain was struggling against the time that flows too fast or too slow, when one has a goal to achieve, someone to meet, a place to go to. He remembered how aware he had become of when Father would run his brain upgrades at the Platform. He had also noticed that Father talked to him more than to other clones. He realised he always wanted to spend longer listening to Father. Differently from his brain, he had no purpose now. He was travelling across a universe that had no boundaries. There was no longer a Base to return to.

'Minimum hearth rate level achieved. Danger.' Now EhVA sounded strangely surprised. 'Transmitting emergency signal to Base.'

He did not know whether to laugh or cry. What came out of his mouth was a coughing fit.

'Cannot detect Base signal. Cannot detect...'

Of course she couldn't. They were all dead. In the last message his Father had appeared different from the start. His face was grey. He had not looked straight at the screen. His hands were holding tightly the armrests of his chair. 'The Platform would have never survived without our research,' he began. He stopped and breathed in deeply. 'We had to try and experiment with genetically modified organisms,' he continued. Another pause, another deep breath. '...to produce heat resistant carbon fibers for construction...'

He seemed unable to speak '...and as a source of energy.' It was as if he was in pain and each word was hurting him. 'We have failed,' he finally added while raising bloodshot eyes and looking straight at him from the other side of the solar system. The creatures, he had explained, had colonized the Platform. Speeder he had said. Spider? Another of those Earthling terms for objects and forms of life he had never seen. Whatever it was, It was also hissing behind Father's door. Father said he would cut off and start the destruction procedure for the whole Platform. It was the first time he had ever called his name. 'Adam,' he had said. His heart had pounded so fast he almost could not remember the rest of the message. He thought Father had said again something about Earth and that there was a mission he should accomplish. But what was the point now?

He had been sent looking for 'living space' for the Platform. A colony of 5,000 human beings living on an artificial structure, which was running out of resources. They needed a planet. But they had run out of time. And it was only crumbles of time and space that were left now. A layer of titanium as thick as a wrist that separated his safe space from the Thing. One and a half leg length that would have stood between the chair and the door once It managed to get through. The space between the chair and the back of his head, or leg, or arm, or whatever It would have reached first. In the infinity of the galaxy, that was the only distance that now mattered.

The Thing had to have been living there for a while. Adam had heard scratching noises. He had seen glass-like fibers under the bridge to the engine rooms but foolishly assumed it was space moss. He should have analyzed it. On mission time unit 8,714, after the last time he had eaten, he went to harvest the in vitro muscle tissue and found that half the lab had been destroyed. The protein ratios had been devoured and there was a hole in the ventilation system. He had sat on the cold floor, he did not know for how long. He had stared at the glass shards. He had touched the twisted tops of the steel tables. It was as if they had been torn apart by giant fangs.

It had to be a big creature. Why had its presence not been detected? Had it destroyed the defence system? Or was it because it was already onboard when he had left the Base? There was another possibility. It had happened before at the Platform. A space-engineered clone like him had killed some of the other Fathers while pursuing some intruder nobody else could see, then destroyed itself. When Father was informed about it he had stared at the floor without blinking. 'That's how it will all end,' he said after a very long pause and before covering his face with his hands.

Adam had decided to search the pod and was rushing to area 7 to get a Directed Energy Weapon. But the Thing found him first. As soon as he rounded the corner to the central deck he saw It at the end of the corridor, with all of its legs, eyes and keratine claws. It was double his size. Although it was not mechanical, it looked perfectly designed for survival. It spouted a thick string of what looked like liquid silicone at him. He moved away but it glued to his foot and calf burning like melted plexiglas. The substance started liquefying the boot and corroding into his skin. He could see the liquid substance solidifying against the raw flesh, which was sizzling and bubbling beneath it. The liquid was obviously designed not to cut through the prey's limbs, but to weld itself to them in an inescapable grip. The thing had then started methodically folding the string as if it was a cable and was pulling him closer and closer. He knew there was no point resisting. He reached for his laser knife and with a single movement cut his own foot off, then threw the burning blade at the thing, aiming for the eyes' cluster. The thing retreated all of its legs with a loud screech and collapsed on its back while the whole floor shook.

He knew he had only a few instants before the Thing would be on him again. He barely managed to reach the first door, the control room, crawling on his hand, mechanical arm, and right leg. As the titanium door clenched behind his back the Thing crushed on it screeching and repeatedly throwing its whole weight against it. It had spouted its acid silicone against it. The door frame had first made a fizzling sound, like that of sewage being purified by titratable iodine. Then the lights had gone out. The acid was eroding its way into the control room. It was just a matter of time until the door's resistance would be crushed. The Thing was just waiting for that to happen.

That was last time he had been fully conscious. He had considered that the Thing might make its way to the control room through the skeleton of the pod, but maybe, like the formicidae who blindly kept on rebuilding their refuge, its strength was not proportional to the size of its brain.

'Intelligence,' his Father had told him while strapping sensors to his chest during the last biology check before launch, '...is what enables to human species to control the environment,' he continued while examining Adam's eyes and ears with a thin medical torch. 'Science can control the universe,' he said with a look of satisfaction that seemed as much related to his conclusion as to Adam's physical state. It was long afterwards, in one of the last messages from the Platform, after Adam had reported that he still had not detected any habitable planet, that Father explained to him 'the great irony.' Father's head had sunk between protruding shoulders. His forehead was crossed by deep lines. 'Despite our advanced technology, we are just fragile machines,' he had said. Adam could understand. The body was but a vulnerable biological system, too dependent on nutrients, oxygen and water being fed at regular times.

'Good morning.' Had he been asleep? Everything sounded muzzled. His mouth was dry. It was cold. His mechanical arm would not move. The hissing sound had gone. Or was he so used to it he could not hear It anymore? Was the Thing still there?

The hissing sound returned, as if sensing his return to consciousness. That was somehow comforting. At least he knew where It was.

An asteroid appeared on the screen and as quickly disappeared from it. In the fraction of an instant in which the black figure filled the screen the room got even darker and Adam saw his own reflection. Despite the last energy draining out of him his sight still collected enough data for his brain to formulate three final thoughts. He was wrong. There was not just one Thing on the pod. There were two.

RICHARD SMYTH

Deep

Wet, cropped grass. A yellow wagtail: dapper little thing. The sunlight is milky and intermittent. They told me to go deep; I'm deep. Deep fine leg, I think, although I can never remember which of these damn field placings is which.

Out of harm's way: that's the main thing, I suppose. I can hardly see the stumps from here. I might be deep but you couldn't say I'm meaningful.

The wagtail patrols the boundary rope.

Of course, I wonder, sometimes, why I bother with this nonsense at all. Wait – before angry cricket-bats fall upon me, I should define my terms: by nonsense, I don't mean the game, I don't mean cricket. I mean – well, I mean me. Does it matter whether I am on this side of that boundary-rope, in whites, or on that, in slacks, shirtsleeves and a casually-knotted tie? Answer: to the team, to the Emily Second XI, no, not one jot – but to me – me, here, ninth man in, plier of right-arm military medium two or three times a season – the man at deep fine leg – to me, yes, it bloody does.

A lot of them play because they're good at it. Which you can't say is unreasonable. Red-headed Cowper, there, say, hunkered keenly at point – or Dipesh, the skip, the bearded sage at second slip – these boys play for the seconds because they want to play for the firsts, and then they'll play for the firsts because they want a county call-up, or a first-class cap, or just a move up a division or two, to Cankerbridge, maybe, or to Oughtbury –

The older players, meanwhile, come for the beer and the banter (and they don't like it, I'll tell you, when I'm back on my bicycle and away home even before the first round in the clubhouse has been got in, or stood up, or however it is it works).

Frankly, I think some of the others – well, I shouldn't say so, but I think some of the others are only here to try and impress girls. There are some – three, to be exact, in blowy skirts, ponytails, light knitted springtime scarves – over by the third man boundary. Young Gulliver's out there.

And what if I were over there, too, in my shirtsleeves, in my casually-knotted tie?

No daydreaming. Dipesh said that when he sent me out here: no daydreaming, he said, and winked, and patted me on the backside with his sunhat. I know what you're like, he said.

Well, I'm really rather sure he knows no such thing.

I believe that, back in those days, I batted at seven – that is, back when I was, what, twenty-odd, and she – well, I don't know how old she was, and it isn't – wasn't – the done thing to ask.

'Was that good bowling or bad batting?'

I was unbuckling my pads on the grass in front of the pavilion.

'What? – I – '

'Or it could've been bad umpiring, I suppose.'

Automatically I said: 'The umpire is always right.' It's the sort of thing you'd expect an idiot to say, a prig, a buffoon – but she laughed.

I remember that she had her back to the sun and, from where I sat on the grass, looking up at her, she was just a shadow, a deep shadow but a shadow with its own corona – and I remember that she had in her hand a glass of something through which the sunlight refracted.

'Why are you looking at me like that?' she said. I must've

been squinting something rotten – because of the sun, you see.

'Sorry.' I got up, one pad on and one pad off, and blinked, and remembered to smile, and said: 'How do you do? I'm James. It was rank bad batting, I'm afraid.'

'Teresa. Tess,' she said.

I would like to describe her – but if I did I would feel like a scorekeeper. If I were to list, say, the colour of her eyes, the way in which she pinned up her hair, her accent (which at first I couldn't place), the cut of her dress – well, it would make me feel like a statistician.

And besides, it isn't as though, if I don't enumerate these things, if they aren't listed, it isn't as though they weren't there, it's not as though they didn't happen.

There's a clunk from the square and there goes Cowper, haring after the ball – swoops, turns, coils and uncoils and slap it goes into the keeper's gloves. A single.

'How many are there still to go?'

'Three,' I said (as I mentioned, I batted at seven in those days). 'That is, three wickets. Four batsmen. Or, well, the two batting now, that is, and two more.'

'I expect that makes some sort of sense.'

'You aren't bored with it?'

'Oh.' She looked over her shoulder. Lowell, the number five, prodded away a full one from their big quick. Then she looked back at me. 'Bored would be a strong term,' she said.

'Disenchanted, possibly?' I ventured, and she laughed again.

At that time, I didn't know anything about disenchantment.

Tess told me that she was there because her brother, Christopher, was a batsman for the opposing team. Their third man in – their best player.

'You bowled him out,' she said.

'Sorry,' I said, though I wasn't. I remembered the ball. It had been a devilish off-cutter that pegged back his middle stump with the scoreboard showing twenty-two for two.

'I don't care,' she said. 'Besides, he's insufferable when he makes a big score.'

Christopher's still alive. I don't know if he still plays; we aren't really in touch any more. I watch the man at the crease stride forward to meet the ball and in a gesture of fuid, flanneled equipoise sweep it to the boundary. Dipesh shouts a word of encouragement to our pink-faced bowler.

There is a sort of enchantment to it, to what we do here (or at least to what we try to do here). When it works, I mean. A sort of magic. When you have the feeling that time and motion, after spending so long obstructing you, fighting you, are all of a sudden with you, and fighting on your side – when the bat swings or the ball leaves your right hand and it is as though you are watching something you have seen before, a replay or repeat, and you are able to say to yourself, quite calmly, yes, I knew that that's how it would go – I knew that it would turn out that way.

As one gets older one gets less good at cricket and so one learns a little about disenchantment.

'Perhaps you'd like another drink?' I said.

She replied, with a smile: 'Perhaps I would.'

And of course I could go on – every word, every laugh, and then, later, every touch and every kiss – all of it carefully noted, inked in, and then, why not, totalled up, too: yes, let's see what the two of us made, in the end.

Why do I bother with this nonsense? There are shouts and commotion as the batsmen scramble two.

We were married, me and Tess, at the end of that summer, in the Methodist chapel on the other side of the road from the cricket-field. My father's father had been a lay preacher in that dissenting faith; it was still, more or less, my father's religion. It rained on the day but no-one gave a damn (save for the minister, who had bicycled from Cankerbridge).

Tess wore wildflowers. The second eleven formed a laughing guard of honour outside the chapel, cricket bats held high in the rain – and then, with a cold spread and seltzer toasts waiting for us at Emily Hall, not to mention my father and mother and the sodden minister, Christopher (fashioning an umbrella from his sweater and elbows) led Tess and me and the cricketers across the road, to the Shepherd's Arms. We drank glowing brown bitter. In fact I drank three pints of glowing brown bitter. Tess drank a glass of inexpensive white wine and when we left she left her wildflowers behind.

'You'll just have to pick me some more,' she said.

'I don't think you're allowed to, you know,' I said, idiotically. 'I think they have laws about it, or by-laws, or something. You aren't supposed to pick them, or else they'll all die out. If everyone went around picking daisies, there wouldn't be any daisies left.'

'Well, I wouldn't want that,' Tess said, and took my hand, and folded her fingers between mine.

Here in the outfield there are daisies beneath my feet. If Dipesh were out here he'd dash them with his boots and curse the groundskeeper. I just leave them be.

A chaffinch is singing in an elder just beyond the square-leg boundary. The song of the chaffinch has been likened to the approach and delivery of a fast bowler: the galloping run-up (pa-pa-pa-pa-pa), the rhythmic convulsion at the wicket (papapa) and then wheee (the hurtle of the ball down the pitch) –

It all seems terribly easy for the chaffinch. The chaffinch, I suppose, doesn't know that there are times when singing isn't easy, when you simply can't sing – when there simply isn't a song to be sung.

I don't suppose that the chaffinch will ever find out

otherwise. When I was young, and when Tess was young, I barely knew more than that chaffinch does. I, however, did find out otherwise.

'I'm sorry, old man,' Christopher said, resting his hand on my elbow, at the funeral.

I remember thinking: you shouldn't say that. You shouldn't say 'old man' when you are an old man – and the person you're talking to is an old man, too.

I said: 'It's just unfair. That's all. It's like when you play and miss and the wicket-keeper and the slip fielders all appeal and the umpire says you've edged it and you know damn well you haven't edged it, but there's nothing you can do about it, you're not even supposed to say anything, when you want to say, no, I didn't edge it, you're wrong, it's not fair, it's not fair – and you can't. All you're supposed to do is walk off the field. As if you don't even mind.'

Christopher squeezed my arm. I knew that other people in the room were looking at me, because I suppose I must have raised my voice. I knew, too, that Christopher didn't give a damn about that, tall Christopher with his classical off-drive and reckless blond hair. White hair, now – like mine.

'But you didn't play and miss, Jim,' he said.

It was silly and childish, I realise, that we could express our feelings only through the terminology of a bat-and-ball game. Tess would have laughed at us. But still: I understood, this way, that Christopher understood – that he knew what enchantment feels like.

'You absolutely middled it,' Christopher said with a smile.

In the winter-time, the off-season, I can still feel the weight of the cricketball in the palm of my hand – through the winter my hand holds the ache from the caught ball, and my fingertips the feel of the seam, just as my left arm, my left leg, somehow keep in them the gather-and-step of delivery – after-images, you could call them – like the sun you see when you close your eyes on a summer's day.

You couldn't call them feelings. Memories of feelings, perhaps. But, if you remember how it felt, doesn't it mean that somehow you still feel it?

I'm watching the wagtail browse for gnats when there's a sharp noise at the wicket and I look to see the batsmen swivelling on his back foot, his bat slewing high in the wake of a botched cut-shot.

'Catch!'

'Who's there?'

Well, I am, of course. Here in the deep. I lift my face to the sun and frame my fingers against the sky. The sky, looked at that way, seems very small.

Claire Stephenson

River Girl

The drought is ending.

The river rages as you would have never seen. Although, as you remember, it always flowed. Even when the fields were cracked and dusty. Even when small children and cattle resembled little more than brittle cages, skin failing to hide our misfortune.

Before this came you still ached to leave. Sitting on the river bank, chin resting on bony knees, fingers and toes gradually working the packed baked soil into sand, you would look across the green water. The river, wide as our village, was never crossed. Nothing but the plain of Masoti until land and sky met in a shimmering line of heat. For eight years you had seen boats come round one bend in the river and disappear around the next without stopping here. The cargo, under tarpaulin, always looked round and full. The men's skin gleamed like black okja fruits, not like ours which was indistinguishable from the ground underfoot.

When you were playing with the other girls you would always stop to watch the next boat go by. Sometimes when we were bathing you would float on your back and let the current slowly drag you a short way. When you were only three or four you first began to get the feel of the river. I always had to keep one eye on the washing and one on you. I would grasp your ankle and you would lose concentration to come up spluttering but always you would make your way back. Then, at the hut we would go about our chores.

My silence never bothered you. When playing with the other children your voice often rang out above everyone else's. It was big enough for both of us. We always got along much better than other mothers and daughters did. There was an unspoken communication between us. We were alone and at a disadvantage and we had to make things go on.

Only now do I wish I could have told you things.

But I would still have left it too late. You were eight years old.

Everyday we would go and watch the sunset by the river. Like a girl I would sit with you, arms around each other's waists. Your head resting on my shoulder you would talk. Murmuring like the water, a stream of ideas and dreams. But there was one thing I knew. No matter how much the world beyond our village beckoned to you, that even when you grew into a woman you would never leave me or leave without me. The colours would reflect from the water onto us. Our skins fiery red, orange and purple until we became part of the river. We were one together and a part of something bigger. These were the happiest times of day.

When I fell ill you still went to watch the sunset and you would come back and tell me how beautiful it was, although it was as familiar to us both as ourselves. Then you would sit in the darkening shadows by my pallet and whisper until I drifted to sleep.

One night you didn't come back.

That night my fever broke and at first light I made my way to the river. My head was swimming. I felt sick. The journey took a long time and you weren't there. I had hoped to find you sleeping under the one tree where we always sat. But nothing.

I saw someone come out of a neighbouring hut. I couldn't make out who it was but I waved frantically. I began towards the figure but I must have passed out.

When I awoke they told me you had been found a little down river tangled in some weeds. I cried my silent tears as they told me how a passing boat must have stopped. You always smiled at the men on the boats. I never thought they would not see the little girl next to me. You were growing up.

In my dreams I see your face as it was. Only sometimes do I see the gashes you will never wonder at. Gashes you nor I could ever explain.

I dream of you smiling. Bathing in the river that was your grave and friend. I am always glad of this, although sorry too. That your initiation was so cruel.

One day I will join you floating amongst the riverweed and fishes. I dream of the source and the sea and it is all you. My daughter.

And now the drought is ending.

So much water from my eyes.

Claire Stephenson

found art

condensation on the window pane
my view outside today is abstract
bands of colour
a misty Rothko

bright brick red paint on the window frame outside
the dull actual brick of the wall
grass green
evergreen
slate grey
pale sky

a diffuse painting
found art

CLAIRE STEPHENSON

Untitled 1

Hanging from branches

raindrops twinkle

in and out of existence

near the streetlight

In the sky

birds appear

from nothingness

riding the current

then gone

Zodwa Nyoni

Big Daddy's Politiks

Masqueraded as contemporary
Ugandan apostle/revolutionist
An 8 year old with a 15 year old's body.
Breasts 36 Cs enticed:
Effendi's 3 militia soldiers,
9 guerrilla forces,
And 4 coercive commanders.
Regimented urges of do me, Do me! DO ME!!!
Foreshadowed maternal deprivation.
Regular night rotations created,
16,425 different, sexual experiences on the dirty grit:
Every thrust stealing away a piece of what was once
Her benign youth
She felt pain,
She felt guilt,
She felt abandoned,
She felt chained,
She felt abused,
She felt a duty;
A duty to those men, a duty to their cause... to be nothing
But just their whore. She was another girl
Smudging antibody invaders in between her thighs.

Memories played.
Midnight walks never ended at daddy's door;
In mama's forgiving arms or on bended knees,
In front of the pastor's congregational redemptions.

Some of you not girls
You will find it hard to understand:
She had to fight to break free,
She had to lie to break free,
She had to caress, and then kill to break free.
She had to struggle to break free.
Thoughts of breaking free, never brought satisfaction,
She had to sacrifice others to break free.
The unknown was the free but; freedom dreaming was no longer a fear

Child sacrifice mentality knew
To each was still his own. Her hush baby,
She could not let be assassinated.
Tightly gripped AK47 ridges drew blood palm;
Cattle field playgrounds flashed;
Survival instinct jerked a magazine of rounds;
Young girls SCREAMED! She could not be everybody else's leader
Whilst frantically pacin', trippin', fallin',
Standing up on the end
Of what symbolised his reign over her,
Big Daddy aka Idi Amin had pulled the gun on her.
Dusty sunsets flashed.

Heart of an angered pit-bull,
Strength of a baby's first running steps.
All it ever was was a pity.
A pity she, was born,
A girl.

ZODWA NYONI

Youth Service Camps: the inside story

Marching as graduates; they powered
Clad in green fatigues, red-and-green berets
Black combat boots exploding the dirt beneath their feet
and AK47's raised in gun salutes
The Green Bombers of the New State
Compulsory Education System marched
On dusty roads exposing education at its best,
In a truly Zimbabwean manner
Singing revolutionary songs, chanting
'Long live Robert Mugabe!'
'Down with whites!'
'Down with Morgan Tsvangirai!'
'Down with Britain!'
'Down with America!'
Expelling the demons of the West
Renouncing allegiance to the opposition
Proving their loyalty

Regiments of former prefects,
Head boys and head girls
Underachievers and over achievers
Sons and Daughters of Ncube's, Dube's, Moyo's
Makoni's, Shoko's and Zondo's
Paraded diplomas in diplomatic brutality
And coercive liberation achieved with

Study guides of:
How to make gasoline bombs,
How to set up roadblocks
How to detain and terrorize,
How to intimidate and mobilize
How to hate Zimbabweans: Whites and blacks
And How to maintain Mugonomics; by hook or by crook!
In place of Marechera, Hove,
Vera and Dangarembga

During graduation they danced
The dances of the un-redemptive power of violence
Over the gates of white colonialist
They planted illegal colonies on bought land.
Ransacked and burned the very land
Their teachers coveted
Burnt unpatriotic tongues speechless
Eliminated black labourers
Who protected their puppeteers
Forced their mothers, sisters,
Distant aunties and cousins over boarders
To be burnt by karma's guise of xenophobia
Under lit mattresses and beg for mercy
On bended knees at the ends of machetes

They were ruthless
They were the soil on which fears grew
They were made to hate themselves
They were made to hate us
They were made to hate change
They were made to hate the past
They made to hate the truth
They were made to follow orders
They were made
By one man

By one voice
By one fist
By one leader
They were made.

Joshua Byworth

Remkear

Freya was the one who planned the whole trip. She told how me much money we'd need to save, what injections we'd need to get and what stuff I'd have to pack. Once I asked her why I needed a visa when I already had a MasterCard. She just laughed and pulled me to her.

In the weeks before we left, Freya never parted with Cambodia guidebook. I bought her the brand new, full colour edition especially. After dropping out of university, she got a job in this American-style diner called Benny's – the kind of place that brings out cakes with sparklers in them and sings Happy Birthday to the customers. She told me that she used to bring the guidebook with her to read during fag breaks by the bins out back. When she stayed over, she would sit up in bed and flick through it, folding down certain pages. Occasionally, she'd grab the remote to mute whatever programme I was watching so she could read bits out to me. I could never keep track of where she was talking about. But that didn't matter as she twiddled her hair and scrunched her forehead, stumbling over the pronunciation of some must-see place.

Our flight was at twenty past five in the morning, which meant, according to Freya, that we had to be at Heathrow by two. Her mum, Caroline, insisted on dropping us off. The little blue Volkswagen pulled up just before midnight. Mum gave me one last hug, then pushed me from her and held me firmly at arm's length.

'Mind yer-self Matt,' she said.

'Course I will Mum,' I replied.

After giving her a quick peck on the forehead, I slung the backpack over my shoulder and hurried to the car.

'Hi Caroline, thanks for the lift,' I said as I chucked my bag in the backseat and jumped in after it. She looked back at me through the rear view mirror. Freya span round in her seat to look at me, beaming with excitement. She was wearing comfy clothes for the journey. Tracksuit bottoms and my old navy-blue hoodie.

'Got everything?' she asked as we pulled off down the street.

'Everything on your list,' I replied.

She blew me a kiss silently and wriggled back round to sit properly. I looked up to catch Caroline's eyes darting away from the mirror and back onto the road.

The M40 was practically ours at that time of night. Just the odd long-haul lorry driver. But you wouldn't have guessed how late it was by the way Freya was chattering on. How long do you think the check in will be? I wonder what movies they'll have on the plane? What time of day will it be when we get there? It was nice to see her like this. After a while, I leaned up against my backpack. Freya's whiskey-coloured hair was all tied up into a bunch on top so I could see the downy strands at the top of her neck. Watching them, I dozed off.

* * *

Freya looked out at the view as Matt scuffed his way up the steps of Wat Phnom. The temple was situated slap bang in the middle of the capital, surrounded by a typically chaotic southeast-Asian road. Mopeds carrying whole families performed white-knuckle stunts, weaving through the traffic. And the air was filled with the howling of horns.

Hundreds of people milled around the fringes of the

temple grounds. At the entrance, women sold jasmine garlands and bunches of red, hairy fruit that Freya had never seen before. Further in there was a crowd of tourists, desperately waving bananas in the face of a disinterested looking elephant tethered to a nearby tree. Freya had read that it was a runt from the King's personal herd. To their right, a group of women squatted next to large wire cages bustling with small birds, promising good fortune to those who paid to release one. Gangs of macaques sat in the trees above them all, waiting to jump down and snatch any food that was momentarily left unguarded. The temple itself was perched atop the small hill in the centre of all this commotion. Freya looked up at the duck-egg blue stupa that pointed elegantly skyward.

Matt reached the top of the steps. Putting his hands on his hips, he squinted up at the temple and then back down the hill.

'Cool,' he said. 'Should we go then?'

'What?' Freya replied. 'Where to?'

'I don't know, get a drink or something. I think I can see a bar over the road there.'

Freya looked at Matt. He was as pink and shiny as he had been since they arrived a week ago. Without the gel that he used at home, his strawberry blonde hair flopped lifelessly across his face. He flicked his head back to unstick it from his brow.

It reminded her of the night that he had driven all the way up to Leeds to take her home. It had been early, while the others in her halls were still asleep, and had pissed it down all morning. She had just lain on the bed while he packed everything up. It had taken him a few trips to get all the boxes to the car and by the time that he carried her out, his hair was wet through and drips trickled down his face. While they waited for the heating to de-fog the windscreen, she had reached back to grab a towel from one of the boxes and dried his forehead for him.

'Sure,' she said. Drawing her sarong tight across her shoulders, Freya brushed past Matt and headed back down the steps. The slap of his flip flops followed close behind her.

* * *

Freya and Matt had spent three weeks travelling around Cambodia. They had done all those things that Freya had circled in the guidebook. They had ridden the bamboo train through the rice paddies just outside Battambang. They had eaten freshly caught crab in Kompong Som, sprinkled with lime and the local Kampot pepper. They had taken a boat trip to see the floating villages on the Tonle Sap. And, of course, they had seen the sun rise behind Angkor Wat.

They were now back in Phnom Penh. Both of them knew the plan for the next day. At three o'clock in the afternoon a tuk-tuk would arrive at their hotel to take them to Pochentong International Airport. At twenty past five they would get flight FD3617 to Suvarnibhumi Airport in Bangkok. After 2 hours in transit, they would board flight PG4014 and arrive back in Heathrow Terminal 2 at half past two in the morning. Local time.

For their final evening, Freya had persuaded Matt that they should go and see something cultural. After consulting the battered, dog-eared guidebook, they found a place not far from them that staged Khmer shadow puppetry. A quick change and a smear of mosquito repellent later, and they were off.

The Chatamouk Theatre was a grand name for the small building at 166 Sisovath Road. It was a detached, two-storey, former house and one of the many remnants of French colonisation that were scattered across the city. A very long time ago, it had been the home of Jean-Francoise

Adenot, a spice merchant who had made the voyage from his birthplace in Brittany after receiving a letter from a friend of his, who wrote of the beauty and luxury of life in the Orient. Jean-Francoise passed away from dengue hemorrhagic fever a year after he arrived. The building had passed through countless owners since then, until 1994, when an association of Khmer artisans bought it as the base for their performances. When they moved in, they had brightened up the place with a coat of dusky pink paint. But by the time Matt and Freya arrived it was faded, cracked and peeling.

The performance area had been created by knocking down a wall between the living and dining rooms. A tiered row of ten long, wooden benches descended toward a large white screen that was pulled tight across the stage, glowing from the light behind. It was pokier than Matt had imagined. But Freya was delighted, remarking on how intimate it felt. They shuffled their way to the end of one the benches and looked through the programme they had been given at the door.

The show that night was a performance of an ancient Sanskrit epic that the programme described as 'a tale of love and duty played out in the world of giants, monkeys, princes and princesses.'

The lights dimmed. The warped silhouettes of figures hurrying into position flickered over the screen. The traditional Pin Peat orchestra began to play and the shadows of two delicately carved leather figures burst onto the screen. At that moment, neither Matt nor Freya dared to think of home. They just sat and watched as the shadow-lovers danced.

DAN ANNETT

[Untitled]

      am i
a thing-in-myself ?
, the dust smooth-slide upon /
                    / the shelf ?
either   or
that   and   there
this   now
this is my   /   these are my

       on
note(s) ~~of~~ the s(h)elf

from   a [   ] gabion wall
of   a voice,
heavy, hollow
like a footnote
to a project.
but how to pronounce
a   silence (.) ?
- stagger the s -
  words of its standing,
foxed with bags of over
                    spilling
tops, trims darkness
to a dy
      – ing
art.
the rigid roar of a
silence which eats
at its wanders   pulling
                          the
            push,
hungry for -
ward   with pattern.

i am a   part
        apart.
pommel of

            no
every thing
    something

martyr of mileage
the   in
- adaptable ideology
 of the weather
uncurled~ing
        palmettes of a skull
licked.
the trumped tra(m)p
like the matador who dreams himself.

is this a sadman's land
                scape ?

impression

     from blue to blue falling
         from azure to obscure
a brambled body of
       lead-laden legs leading
 a cavalcade of cloud
  to cease the sunlight
   on the brine   for
              a moment

your eyes are a flock of steam,
cogs in water,
quite still.
  born to love a disguise,
    and let the reel fray
        its ties -
            a tongue of paisley silk.

            stretch out your hand:
            let me hold it.

battered bodies take the floor.
    the looseness in limbs
that I can only envy.
    is it the head or is it the hand,
that measures out the stone and
            the sand?

            stretch out your hand:
            let me hold it.

like a lash in the eye,
spathe of a mellowing
mantra,
dead
-quick
danger
  deliberately darting
    down,
like an idea like the cold
shaft at the back
of the head,
old man and all the words that
cannot be
said.

                              stretch out your hand:
                              let me hold it.

toujours
too sure of the facts-
            a curse for contingency-
to be trued,
a collop,
a cataract,
like some pulpit Pushkin
riser, raiser-
chasing the sun.
must the universal be uniform?

                              stretch out your hand:
                              let me hold it.

        isolate
insulate,
crutch calling.
limp is the light
  in the dog-bark dark.
language is the obsolete
                absolute.

                              stretch out your hand:
                              let me hold it.

heads roll
        nod necessary
as pumpjacks in the silk of the
                7pm sulk;
dusk showing.
dust being.
mechanic men of mountains.

　　　　　　　　　　stretch out your hand:
　　　　　　　　　　let me hold it.

an ouroboric world,
　　　authored world,
the cog, the chain, or sprocket?
erring,
　　errorfull
　　　　eros,
stiffly stubborn-
　(en)riched in (en)closure-
lean on
　　　a line,
reconcile the creator
and the destroyer.

　　　　　　　　　　stretch out your hand:
　　　　　　　　　　let me hold it.
　　　　　　　　　　stretch out your hand,

and let me live.

fingers fold, hold,
    bones, (to) balance (to) break
words like a fist.
The hewed heart drops
    like mercury,
        wind scaffolds
            umbrella, eyelids, bone,
                brain.

        melt in my maw my moans,
            spooled on the striated scrub
                of the day.

ramped with
    footsteps like a
coda (like a coda),
  legs of chalk
      carry the black pole of the pool
         below
        looped with, in,
        within
seats of sound.

testicles like a chatelaine.
    to hold yourself
up
suspended size of a
sin, skein,
sewn round
folds,
    rolls
of larded skin,
    sin,
bunds of
    a body

    of
bunds
in the bare-black
    back
    beetle
of the day;
with bowled eyes,
the punctum
  nail of needs,
and the flue feeds the flee.

where are those the broke the night,
bombed it tight
  with tomes and tones
    of time -
people of the pavement,
  the channeled white
    collar of your face(s) -
      casking
cold places

fingers snatch and
 snitch the dance;
and you; upon your
 penrose triangle,
thrift with
your steps.

the stagnant haste
  of the horologist
   wakes,
the I
teased placed
among fingers.

AJ KIRBY

Extract from *Prometheus City*: A Leeds Crime Novel

'Alex'

Rained earlier. Downpour had cleared the air.

Alex wished it was still raining.

Recently, if she'd had a bad night at the poker, the walk of shame had only taken her from sofa to fridge. There she'd take a long slug of coke, straight from the bottle, whilst trying not to notice the designer wine rack. From there to the en suite shower in the guest room. So she wouldn't wake Heath.

Once she was in that shower, once the hard rain hammered down from the oversized shower head onto the top of her own head, she at least felt she could put a certain distance between herself and her loss.

Now, even as she crossed so many still-wet roads, as she scurried past so many closed doors, as she put a whole city between her and the card table in the back room of the Wrights' club, she could still feel her loss on her like a second skin.

She could have taken a taxi. Had cash at home to pay the driver. But she didn't want to communicate with anyone, even at the level of telling a driver where she lived – the back end of Clarence Dock, the place which was once supposed to be the glitzy face of the new Leeds but was now a half-empty white elephant – or even have to face his inquiring gaze in the rear-view mirror. Didn't have the gumption about her right now to come up with some jovial lie as to why she was still out, on this drowned November night, still dressed as she was in her slinky dress and her heels, and her long – but not quite long enough – coat.

Anyway a taxi wouldn't cut it. This walk would provide the scars which would remind her, when she next got that itch that only a high-stakes game would scratch, that there were alternatives to winning.

As she walked east across the city centre, the process of cleansing the city of its traces of human contact began:

At the bookends on Eastgate, a man in a high-vis vest scrubbing some graffiti off a wall.

At Millgarth police station, that great hulking depression of a building, the chorus of a thousand vacuum cleaners in a thousand vacuum corridors.

At the markets, a squad of shuffling men with huge, metre-wide sweeping brushes criss-crossing the grid of stalls.

Towards the Playhouse, a couple street sweeper vehicles – chubby little things – whirred along the pavements in pursuit of stray chipwrappers and plastic bags caught on the gloaming breeze.

Alex felt as though, if she let up with her relentless pace, she'd be cleaned away too, consigned to yesterday. Could hardly remember stumbling away from the card table in the back room, flailing through the door and into the bar, demanding her gear – her mobile phone, her coat – from the shiny shoed barboy's 'safekeeping'.

Even now, she kept having to check both pockets of her leather coat just to make sure she still had the phone. Even as she clutched it in her sweaty palm, she wasn't sure it was actually the same phone, though some part of her knew it was; had already checked for the in-pouring of last night's messages from Heath.

The ones which hadn't been able to get through to her then. Then she'd been out of reach of both mobile signal and sense.

Checked her watch. 5am. Surely too early for Heath. He was generally a late-riser. Generally it was all she could do to get a grunt out of him from underneath the pillow which he'd wedge over his head to block out 'her noise' as she got ready for work.

A see you later love, was a very good day. Generally. But Heath could also be counted on to be the most infuriatingly stubborn man known to humanity.

Which meant there was a very real possibility he'd be up, drumming his fingers on the breakfast bar, waiting for her return. He'd have had an uncharacteristic shave too, just to rub it in. Would be fully dressed; that terrible towelling dressing gown of his – he called it his 'poet's scrubs' – nowhere to be seen. As though he was a regular go-getter, the pacemaker in the Leodian rat-run.

Alex was hurrying past the semi-demolished Tetley brewery now. That once grand place – which used to ring out, like some beery cathedral, with the bell-like sounds of clanging barrels; when the wind was right carried all the way down to the flats at Clarence Dock – now reduced to piles of slag. Weirdly, the façade of the office section of the building remained in the middle of all the collapsed brick and concrete, and it lent the whole place an eerie atmosphere: reminded Alex of some building straight out of Chernobyl.

Sans brewery, this part of Leeds had become something of a wind tunnel. Wet gusts of it whipped up the river Aire and bit into her naked legs, crowded around the collar of her leather coat, stung at her face. Teared her eyes, as though this was some taster for the main event, when she really would cry later.

And because her eyes were watering, it took her a while

to register that a car was slicking along in the distance in her general direction. And because of the blurred outlook they gave her, it took her rather longer than usual to ascertain make, and model, and whether it was a taxi or a police car.

There wasn't really anywhere to hide. To her right, the long palisade perimeter fence which ringed the brewery. To her left, the wide road. If she crossed over, headed for the couple low-slung buildings on the other side – a printers and a derelict newsagents – the police would definitely see her.

She'd look as though she was loitering, even though the real streetwalkers were found a few blocks over, past the big Asda head offices, close to the canal, where the city centre gave way to industrial units. David Street.

Alex winced. Pulled out her phone, thinking she'd use it as a prop. Pretend like she was talking to someone. Pretend like she was a lone, stop-out clubber visiting the city, being guided in by some blurry-eyed air-traffic controller, to the latest crash-pad of choice.

Took her eyes off the approaching car a moment, so when it let out a leery, pre-siren whoop, she almost dropped the phone. Her eyes shot back to the car, which was now in mid-transformation from cruiser to flier. Blue lights disco-balled into life. The promised siren blared into life. The car – a Rover – commenced its ten to sixty. But as it shot past her, she saw the two men, bulky in their uniforms, their utility vests, looking right back at her.

Weighing her up, Heathing her down. Scoring her.

One of the bastards waved.

Alex felt the colour rising in her cheeks. The shame like a fist in her throat. She hung her head and let the car pass, and then she walked on.

But now her senses were freshly alert. As she crossed the road, she saw a scruffy brown shape – larger than you'd expect – skittering along the kerbside between gutters. Rat. Might as well have been a beaver. Over the other side, Alex, a chicken-crossed, heard the whir of a CCTV camera, perched above the roller-shutted door to the printers, as it responded to her movements, sweeping in an arc as she passed.

She cut left, following the brown signs which indicated the Royal Armories and Clarence Dock. On one side of her a high wall made of blood-red bricks. On the other the first of the half-empty apartment blocks. A huge coffin of a place containing countless blind windows, countless TO LET signs. Farther along, as residential lets gave way to commercial lets, those scores of glitzy, but empty shops which had been recessioned out of existence, she finally slackened her pace.

The fist in her throat was melting now, and whatever had made it – guilt, embarrassment, shame – now tasted bitter.

They lived in the last block, last after even the student residences, before Clarence Dock became the badlands again. Their flat was on the fifth floor of the strangely-shaped building which was locally known as 'the sail', but was actually named, rather pretentiously, and rather pointlessly, too, 'One', as though it was the one and only.

The Chesney Hawkes of Leodian apartment blocks.

She took a deep, ragged breath, and looked up. Checked for a telltale light on in their flat. But none could be seen. So she let that same breath out again. It whistled through her teeth. Stung her fillings.

Badged into 'One'. Shouldered the heavy door. Cast a glance at the row of numbered post-boxes affixed to the entranceway wall. Saw the thousands of fast food delivery menus and flyers for special nights at the casino spitting out of their box. Couldn't face sorting through them now.

Her mind was even more cluttered than the box, she reckoned.

Lift wasn't working. Course it wasn't: when you trudged the walk of shame, everything seemed to conspire to make those steps feel worse.

Took the stairs. By the time she reached the fifth floor, she'd had to remove leather coat and drape it, a dead soldier, over her arm. And by the time she reached the soft, but heavy, beech door to their flat, she was having to wipe her forehead with her forearm. Then came the losing battle to find her door-key in her clutch bag. Tumbling out receipts, a stray chip, loose coins, a half-consumed packet of chewing gum, a nail-file she couldn't ever remember having used.

Knowing Heath, he'd probably spirited her key out of her bag before she left, or at some other unknown time, just so she'd have to knock-on to announce her arrival. Alex couldn't believe that after everything she'd faced on the way home, she was now going to lose because she didn't have her motherfucking, goddamnit key.

Knocked the door. Four short, sharp raps of knuckle-to-beech. Then stood, shuffling like her feet were a deck of cards, waiting for the door to yawn open.

Waited seven, eight beats.

No answer.

Pressed the side of her face to the oddly warm wood and tried to listen. The door sounding oddly alive as though it was convinced it remained a tree in some forest on the Peak District hills, as though it had blanked out the memory of being lumberjacked down and brought here, into a newer, more concrete forest.

Beyond the door, nothing.

Checked her watch. Heath couldn't have set out for work already. Too early. Nor could she imagine his having slept through her knocking. And he wouldn't be ignoring her. It wasn't in his nature to punish her that way, when he couldn't see her face, when he could have his fill of her, his victory over her, if he simply opened the door to her.

She thought about sliding down the smooth surface of the door. Crashing down onto her buttocks and simply waiting it out. Waiting for him to give in first, because he would. He always did. But then she felt a flash of anger in her stomach.

She stood. Reached for the handle, ready to rattle the hell out of it, ready to shake the living daylights out of it, ready to make it sound as though some goddamn gangster, one of the Wrights' lackeys, was here, ready to shake the place down. If Heath was asleep – tucked safe and warm inside one of his soppy dreams about some airy-fairy future when his poetic fumblings had made him into the famous, special individual his goddamn middle class mummy and daddy always told him he'd grow up to be, and not the snivelling, workshy malcontent he actually was – she wanted him to wake up fearing that Leeds was suffering its first earthquake which would register on the high end of the Richter Scale.

Only, when she touched the handle it gave. She pushed it down and then felt the catch go, and then, as she pushed against its weight, it submitted.

The door was already open.

Instinct kicked in. Her tired mind suddenly whirred into life, performing all kinds of involuntary risk assessments, playing out worst-case scenarios, calculating odds, probabilities.

First thing she did was kick off her shoes. Leave them outside the door. Then, quietly, she stepped inside, letting the door close softly behind her, using her back at a buffeter. Pointless as it was, as she'd already made enough noise to wake even dead poets like Heath, she didn't want to draw any more attention to herself.

She stood, back to the door.

Looked for sore-thumbs, her head tick-tocking round,

eyes travelling over the furry WELCOME mat and over the polished wood floor, where there were no new scuff-marks. Then up, to the long-broken video entry system, to the mostly empty coat-rack which only half masked the awful pen and ink sketch of the two of them together which one of Heath's friends had produced for them as a wedding gift: pair of them grinning like goons in a way they'd never done in real life.

Alex sighed, made like a cat. Poised, compact, springy on her feet, she whispered across the floor towards the first of the doors leading off the hallway. Though she could feel the hairs on the back of her neck bristling she crept towards the open bathroom door, edged her head around it, and stared into the darkness. Gradually picking out the now-defunct heated towel rail, then past it, the toilet, with, as usual, the seat left up. Beyond that the sleek glass of the shower cubicle.

Saw something dark and kind of slumped on the tiled floor and her heart bungeed. Fingers prickly with tension, she stretched for the light-pull. But even as she tugged the cord, her eyes were adjusting and she was registering the fact that this was not Heath, head cracked open by a crowbar, body fallen at an unnatural angle, but was actually a common or garden towel, tossed to the floor in typical Heath fashion après shower.

Backed out of the bathroom. Made for the second door leading off the main hallway. This door led to the main bedroom and she half-expected to see Heath's slumped, log-form under the duvet; half-expected her entrance to be greeted with a heavy snore too. But the room was empty.

And so on to the guest bedroom, where there was not even a crease on the sheets to indicate he'd slept in there to teach her a lesson for her keeping up the nightwatch. Weirdly, the room smelled abandoned, as though it hadn't contained people in it for a long time, though she knew she'd slept in here only a week ago, after the latest row. She closed the door gently, respectfully, as though she hadn't wanted to disturb the room's peace.

Nobody home in the living room either.

She paused. Ran her fingers through her now-greasy hair. Felt them catching towards the front, where she'd been altogether too liberal with the hairspray.

Retraced her steps. Back to the hallway. And this time, she looked on the familiar unfamiliars with practised eyes. And immediately saw what was different.

There, pinned to the back of the front door, where only a few moments ago she'd been leaning, sniffing the air like she was some kind of dirty stop-out guard dog, was the torn wedding photograph. The one they'd had framed – until very recently – and hung in the guest bedroom.

Alex's bare feet slapped against the wood floor as she rushed over to it, as though in a race against time to pull the pin out of the door. As though, in getting there in record time and in touching the pin, she might encounter some kind of remainder of Heath. Heat, or a thick thumbprint left behind.

She pulled the two halves of the picture off the door. Checked the back for some kind of note. But then she realised there didn't need to be a note. The picture said a thousand words. Or just three. It was over.

This knowledge did not hit her like a sledgehammer, nor roil in her guts, nor cause the long-awaited tears to prick the corners of her eyes. She simply registered it, with a shrug.

He'd gone. Only strange thing about it was the fact he'd done the leaving. She'd always figured it would be her who'd be the one to walk away, a slammed door in her wake.

Her mobile buzzed in her pocket like an angry wasp. She checked it. Work.

She was needed.

An emergency, apparently.

Like there wasn't one here.

She thought about ignoring it even as she stumbled into the bathroom and tugged on the light-pull. Thought about the same thing as she tried not to catch her own eyes in the mirror; as she began to shed her skin of the night before, sloughing off parts of herself which were also not of herself. Tearing off her false nails and chucking them in the sink. Yanking off dangly earrings and leaving them on the counter, amongst the hillocks of shaving foam.

Her slinky dress came next.

Then, after a quick, barely restorative shower, she creaked through into the bedroom, seeking out something more comfortable, eventually settling on jeans and a Superdry hoodie which she could lose herself in. Nike Airs which would at least provide some cushioning for her battered and bruised feet.

Next, the kitchen, where she quickly boiled the kettle and washed her mouth out with a slug of bitter, scaldingly hot coffee, then sluiced the rest of the mug down the sink.

And finally, back to the hallway and the telephone table, where she picked up her mobile phone and flat key, her warrant card and badge.

ADAM Z. ROBINSON

Gifted

He stared down the barrel of the camera and confessed it all. He apologised, deeply, through muted sobs, for misleading us. For deceiving every one of us so cruelly. For making a mockery of his mystic art. All lies.

And she watched from the wings. A scorching stare; a poisonous, enthralling smile.

He shook; whether with guilt or with shame or with fear, we could not could tell. The paper in his hand, from which he read, rustled noisily. His eyes told of the threat of vacillation, but he stayed the course of curious repentance. And every now and then she exhaled steadily from her position, just over his right shoulder.

'I have caused the deaths of one-thousand, two-hundred and six animals; large and small. Many perished in unimaginable agony.' His lip quivered. 'A total of seventeen human minds and souls have been lost to my art … my act. These wretches are now with the devil. I am a liar. I am a charlatan. I have masqueraded as a masterful peddler of the wonderful. But I am a vile deceiver. My magic is all illusion. My feats of the impossible, mere theatre.'

The nation drew breath together. Betrayal. The wonder trickled away like so much spoiled, spilt milk. All fabrication and deception and puffs of smoke, now roiling away. And people were angry.

'There is a basement…' His words caught in his throat. He stopped, broke and recomposed himself. 'And that's where the children are. All of them. You see, it was not enchantment but a sham. A show. And they are all there.'

As the camera panned closer – a mechanical gesture of incredulity – the noise of disruption from outside the bolted studio doors began and rose rapidly. A rumble of disquiet, becoming, steadily, a chaos of voices; demanding the return of their trust and they were sharpening their knives.

And in the wings, her smile shrank and a final sigh signified her satisfaction. With him since her youth. Daughter of the first innocent woman who went mad by his trusted hand. This young woman held his secrets like a bouquet and watched them wither with time. And as the doors began to buckle; and just before the anger of the deceived was realised upon the man's feeble, old body; this deathly posy of secrets was handed back to the world. By her.

Wearing the clothes in which he'd dressed and kept her. Revealing, at last, her lucidity. The magician's assistant.

ADAM Z. ROBINSON

Connivance

It is a sacred bond, marriage. A union which tangles the souls and bodies of those wedded to one another. We are each other's keeper. This is something I know.

It is true that I have spent many anxious evenings, after sun down, considering flight; leaving the struggle behind. But as soon as the thought is processed, the wardrobe opened, the carry case half-stuffed with garments, he is home. Freshly-energised and hot with the passing night's potential.

I used to think our nocturnal rendezvous romantic. Passionate and deliberate and different. This otherness, this separation from all I'd know before him, I guarded it fiercely. But that fire has long-since burned out. And he now seeks the company of others in those black hours.

Even our wedding took place under the stars, with only a few insignificant and anonymous witnesses (dead and buried). He is the only man I've ever truly loved.I know that I'm weak to want to leave. There is rationality in his explanations; his confessions; his claims of necessity and survival and of an unslakable hunger. And I begin to accept him all over again. Love conquers.

But then the morning's news comes; another animal's throat has been torn out; some stray has been eviscerated and left on waste land.

And things far, far worse. Things I cannot bring myself to think of. There are so many homeless wretches in this city and I thank Holy God, knowing what I now know, that we have a roof over our heads. Though it seems that he's rarely under it.

I'll keep turning the other way. Both my eyes are blind.

He sleeps through the day.

JENNY BEECH

The Gap in the Curtains

He flicked a switch. Harsh artificial light flooded from the ceiling, illuminating the dusty blinds, the black spots of damp in the corners and the faded formica floor of the bathroom. Will shuffled towards the sink and turning the hot tap, let the tepid flow spill over his fingers. He lifted a pair of underwear, stained with a scarlet streak of blood and ran them under the water, his eyes glazing over as he rubbed them with soap and scrubbed them between his hands. The washing machine could never quite manage to clear bloodstains; most of Jo's underwear was testament to the fact. After a few minutes of washing, with only the hushing of the tap to kill the silence, Will rinsed them clean and placed his hands on either side of the sink, leaning on it heavily. He stared into the bathroom mirror at his permanent frown and the grey hairs that were appearing at his temples and wondered for the hundredth time that day, why he hadn't left his wife and why he felt so guilty for wanting to.

He breathed a long sigh, hung the underwear on a foldout rack behind the door and entered the bedroom.

Jo was in bed. Jo was always in bed. The curtains were drawn and she had turned away from the golden glow of her bedside light.

'Fancy going out tonight?' Will asked in a false, cheery voice. He felt sickened at himself for saying it. She didn't answer.

Jo's greasy hair was splayed across the pillow, beneath

the bed sheets her body was naked and frail and her eyes, staring blankly at the opposite wall, seemed hollow. If she wasn't breathing she could've passed for dead. For a split second Will contemplated the freedom that he might feel if she just slipped away...

What was he thinking? His eyes filled with tears of remorse and frustration and he turned to the wall so that Jo wouldn't see. The last thing he wanted was to upset her. He took another deep breath and knelt beside the bed.

'Jo?' he whispered softly. He cupped her face in his hands and moved to kiss her but her lips were lifeless beneath his and she turned her head away. Will let go. He stroked and kissed her matted hair and got to his feet.

He stripped back the bedsheets and Jo didn't protest, she didn't even move. She hardly ate these days and her body had grown thin; so different from the soft curves and the bright-eyed smile of her former self. Will filled a washing up bowl with soapy water and a flannel and started to wash her down with firm, gentle strokes. She remained silent and unresponsive, even when he turned her over and washed between her legs. He felt a bittersweet mixture of compassion and despise.

The doctor had examined her more than once but the diagnosis had been the same; it was a sickness of the mind, not the body. A course of antidepressants had done little to help and suggesting a psychiatrist had provoked a violent reaction from Jo. He had a sudden flashback Jo huddled into a corner, staring at him wide-eyed and terrified as if he were the devil himself. Will hadn't even minded; any reaction was better than this stale silence.

He cleaned the room, tied back her hair, lined her underwear with a fresh sanitary towel, dressed her in a nightie, hoovered the floor and emptied the overflowing washing basket. The only time Jo made a sound was a small, pathetic whining noise when he had opened the curtains. She hadn't stopped until he had closed them again. He returned every day from work to find that Jo had barely moved and it had been the same for the past two years.

He considered going out but knew that he would only feel guilty for leaving her so he went downstairs to watch television, just to hear the sound of other peoples voices and returned three hours later feeling just as lonely as he had before.

It was 10pm. He undressed and got into bed beside Jo, pressing himself against her back and kissing her on the space between her shoulder and neck. She wasn't asleep but she didn't move and Will soon pulled away.

On Jo's bedside table there were two pictures; one was face down on the dresser and the other was turned towards her. The one that was turned down was their wedding photo. They had been married in the Autumn of them both being twenty four and the photo showed smooth cheeks, unbreakable smiles and a churchyard scattered with russet leaves. The other photo was of a child with Jo's dramatically dark hair and Will's clear blue eyes.

Jessica, their first and only child, had died three years ago in a car crash at the age of two.

He couldn't remember a time in that first year when he had not been crying. He had found that he could speak to no one but Jo. He had quit his old job and stayed in the house, looking through Jessica's photos, her clothes and toys and birthday cards. His days had been filled with unbearable memories of her laugh, her nonsensical talk and her wide, innocent eyes that had stared into his with such trust and admiration. Jo had become wildly busy after a quiet funeral, spending all hours she could at work, mostly ignoring Will and the well-meaning calls from family. Will warned her to stop and let herself think for a moment but she hadn't wanted to listen. She slowly lost contact with her friends and was spending less and less time in the house until one day, she wouldn't get out of bed. Will ventured from the house for shopping and returned to find that she had taken all of Jessica's old things to the dump, apart from the one picture that now sat by her bedside.

Since then she hadn't left the house and had sunk into a deep depression. He couldn't remember the last time she had made eye contact with him. She spent her days staring at the photo on her bedside table or a blank wall or the small chink of light that fell through the curtains.

Will had been tempted to find another woman, to fill the aching void inside him that his daughter and his wife had wrenched open, but he knew that he couldn't. He had tried to stay away from the house but any enjoyment was tainted by the guilt of leaving her on her own. He had tried to console himself with alcohol but had found that he only grew more lonely. He kept telling himself that had it been the other way round, she would have done the same for him but even that sounded like a lie after these two years of nothing from her. With his wife sleeping in the bed beside him, Will felt like he was the only soul left in the universe. He fell asleep with tired, angry tears soaking his pillow.

It was midnight and Jo was still awake. Something was different tonight but she couldn't summon the energy to work out what. She had heard Will crying on the other side of the bed but had not comforted him. A thick bubble separated her from the world, dulling her senses and although she remembered the bright spectrum of emotions that she had once felt, she was now only numb. She was a hollow shell. Maybe that was just what happened when you grew older? Maybe Will would switch off soon too and they would lie down in the same bed for the rest of their lives... but who would look after her if he did? She frowned slightly before her face fell back into its blank, immovable expression. It didn't matter anyway.

Jo blinked and stared at the gap in the curtains. The hazy orange light from the street lamps was splashed across the bed. She wished the curtain was closed; she hated the idea of the outside world existing behind the window and the thought of others seeing her.

She wanted to ask Will to leave her, there was still a part of her that felt guilty when he looked at her with those sorrowful eyes and she didn't want to feel anything, but she couldn't find the energy to speak.

Jo could remember the first day when she had felt the Numbness settle over her like a dead weight. Just the day before she had been running hard from the manic grief that lingered at the back of her mind and then suddenly, it had overtaken her. She had thought that she would've gone insane with it but instead she felt this... nothingness. She hadn't wanted to do anything anymore. She didn't feel anything, she didn't care about anything and if she hadn't had Will beside her, talking to her, she might've convinced herself that she had already died.

Jo felt a sudden burning in her chest. There it was again, that feeling that something was different tonight. She felt a distant fear; feelings were something that she had managed to cut herself off from for the past two years. She coughed and continued to stare at the chink of light. Hours dragged their feet. Jo rarely slept these days but spent her nights like she spent her days; restless in lethargy; feeling nothing and doing nothing. Will turned in his sleep beside her and she instinctively reached out a hand to him. She frowned again. That was new.

Shuffling around until she was facing Will's sleeping face, she tentatively reached out a hand to touch his arm, staring at the creases at the corners of his eyes.

It hit her hard and sudden. Grief loomed in the darkness, seeping in from every dark corner like the monsters in children's stories. Memories of the crash, of Jessica's face flashed before her, making her cry out. It wasn't the gentle aching of sorrow, this grief, it was huge; it was a chasm that engulfed her, that flooded her with an overwhelming fear. Even two years of dull, grey days was preferable to this. Her eyes flowed with tears like an open wound and she rocked with messy, undignified sobs. Will had woken up now looking confused and as wave after wave of grief crashed over her, her crying became screams.

Two o'clock on a gentle July afternoon found Will inside, holding Jo to him as she sobbed. He had called into work yesterday morning after a fitful night of trying to calm Jo down. He hadn't been able to leave her in this state and had spent over a day trying to comfort her. He hadn't rang the doctor or explained to anyone what had happened. He was following his instincts on this one; she could cry, scream, break things, do whatever she wanted. Admittedly he had been terrified when he had woken up to find her screaming in the bed next to him but he felt strangely hopeful.

Jo looked a mess; her hair was wild, her face was red, her eyes were swollen from crying and the room was in complete disarray from her rampages. Will even had a small bruise on his shoulder where she had hit him. After hours of watching her he had figured that if she was angry then he should leave her to it, just making sure she did nothing to hurt herself and then afterwards, when it became despair and sorrow, he would hold her and rock her like a child. He felt like he had no idea what he was doing but just having some insight, some connection with his wife and being able to do something to help her, was more of a relief than he could describe. She began to sob pityingly, clinging to the front of his t shirt.

'It's alright darling... it's alright...' he had repeated those words until his voice was hoarse. Was it alright though?

Will had no idea. Breathing deeply, he pulled Jo a little closer and decided to cry with her.

Jo remember seeing Will cry like this many times, in that first year after Jessica's death; those screaming, unconsolable sobs. She had despised him for it then, feeling pride at her ability to stay calm and be brave when all along it had been cowardice that had kept her from crying. She felt ashamed now and a deep sympathy for him. It felt like she had woken up to a nightmare; all these uncontainable, terrifying feelings crowding in from all sides, yet she felt even more fear at the thought of sinking back into that dead depression.

After three days, she slept. It was a deep sleep like she hadn't had in years and when she woke up, in the early morning of a thursday, things seemed different. She was no longer crying.

Will was sleeping beside her. She moved close beside him, breathing in his scent and reaching out to touch his sweet, sleeping face. He opened his eyes and a deep sadness and fear broke into his peaceful expression. Jo began to cry again, soft, silent tears rolling into her hair. She leaned in closer and gave him a gentle, lingering kiss.

'Why are you crying Jo?' he spoke with such compassion. It was unbearable to think of the frustration and loneliness and hopelessness that she had put him through but as remorseful tears continued to drip onto the pillow, she knew that she hadn't been able to stop. The world had just been too dark for her to open her eyes and look at it.

'I'm crying because ... I wasn't crying.' She laughed and Will gave her a worried look. 'I mean I woke up today and I wasn't crying and I wasn't sure how to feel about that ... so I cried.'

Will smiled. 'I think I should go into work and explain where I've been for the past three days.' Jo simply nodded.

'Will you still be here when I get back?' his face was serious. Jo nodded again, not quite smiling but no longer frowning. Will moved to get up but Jo caught his arm,

'Will?' She whispered his name into the dark room, sounding like a frightened child, 'I ... I'm just...' she began and found that she had no words. Will nodded as if he had understood, reached down and kissed her. He had a sudden urge to tell her that he loved her but found that he couldn't. Those years of hurt would not fade overnight but for the first time he felt that a wind was blowing the cobwebs from his marriage and that maybe he might be able to tell her again sometime soon. He thought about the words for a while. I love you. They still felt important; heavy somehow, even now. He would savour them for a while. She was no longer the rosy-cheeked, tender-hearted girl that he had once vowed to love but she was still Jo.

He got dressed and exchanged a few words with Jo about small, unimportant things, as if by mentioning it they might scare away this new hope that had inexplicably bled into their lives. On the drive to work, Will found himself thinking about Jo. Not her younger, simpler self but the wild, unpredictable, terribly sad women whom he had left at home in his bed and he found, much to his surprise, that he did love her after all.

He was in love with his wife and he had heard her laugh that morning and all because of those two things, he just about felt like the happiest person alive.

Still in a dirty nightie, having not washed for days, Jo peeled back the covers and stepped out of bed. With the air of one changing the course of the world, she reached towards the gap in the curtains with shaking fingers. In one grand gesture, she swept them open and blinked into the stubbornly bright light of a summer morning. Clouds in honey-coloured clusters hung in the vast expanse of a blue sky. Jo breathed in sharply and resisted the temptation to close the curtains again. It was all so painfully beautiful. She had forgotten that the world could be beautiful.

Jo felt naked beneath the persistent glow of the sun; naked and washed clean and incredibly small. She breathed in, she prayed and she smiled and for a moment she looked like the joyful girl in the wedding photograph that now stood face up on the dusty surface of the bedside table.

LIZZI HAWKINS

A Garden with Birds

I remember when I saw them, five doors down from the
   churchyard,
wheeling in the brittle blue morning like wind-startled
   clouds –
except the sky was clear that day.

They were
spilling up from the ground, like poems
from an open mouth, like cut beads flung
from a necklace, like music escaping its stave.

They were
silent black sonatas, peaking and falling
on a frequency that into, only I was tuned.

A moment, tossing their sonorous secrets to the sun.

Then up, Godwards,
above a village still with sleep,
then a dark graze on the horizon's cheek
then gone.

And I think of myself, decades down the line,
blurred by the spin of passing time,
and wonder if I'll still be here,
standing on the wrong side of fences,
thinking of all that I'd give for a garden with birds.

Lizzi Hawkins

Time Capsule

X marks the spot
where, some months short of seven
we upturned the earth to leave our mark,
dirt-staining our palms for weeks.

4 steps, heel to toe, north of the nettles behind the shed,
2 east of the kitchen window's coloured panes,
3 deep, in uncut grass

we sat
and filled a shoebox,
a doll's bungalow in some past life
reincarnated, at our childish convenience,
as a time machine.

We left:
the lozenge of a two pence piece,
a measure of school hair ribbon,
a wad of newspapers,
the uniform glass eyes
of marbles, a coloured spill
of chalks.

For the discoverer, I threw in a prize –
a white crown, daisy-weft,
that I was still young enough to think
they would pull, fresh

from the box
in a thousand years' time
and wear, like some pale queen
of new beginnings.

To these things we gave
an unmourned grave; wished
them well for
future lives.

Now I am older,
I see our mark is everywhere:
in the stitch of a wound,
strung dark on a rosary
or on the backs of envelopes
bearing bad news.
We were far apart by then

but I still left an X,
mid-month, on my calendar.
Let it blackly erase a day.

Now I am here,
at my feet there is
a different kind of digging.
A farewell more final.
And in the fresh earth there is
a different kind of cross,
one that I do not believe in anymore,

because I know
that you will not be granted
a grand rediscovery,
like we thought that box would get.

So we mark you,
I in this way:

I put white daisies in the ground again,
this time understanding rot.

Lizzi Hawkins

Trauma

He hasn't forgotten
his days of pavement tracing,
the yowling nights of not-sleep
when his body became the margin of the road.
Sometimes he'd wake with boot marks
on the slice of his cheek.

He's still a child in the dark,
is sunk in relief when the sky hum-clicks
and sockets of sodium grimace orange.
He still twitches when hands plunge
for pockets, at the clang of footsteps,
his nerves haven't yet learnt not to lock.

When he first saw pound coins
he thought they were pools of yellow oil
flung from the overhang of a scaffold.
He was used to copper; they were unfamiliar
like kisses, incorrect
like a snowbank in the hot pout of August.

Now, under cold sheets,
his wife fingers the creases of his temples,
tries to soothe the black trauma behind his eyes.
He still won't sleep for fear of waking
on the graveyard slabs of the city,
somewhere that is not here.

LIZZI HAWKINS

Wife

A spring-time marriage,
warm kisses and lilies.
She, a white shiver of joy.

Carried over the threshold,
a key in his smiling mouth.
She, hot tea and cinnamon.

Mute and benign
and aching his absence,
She, snarling her grief to the moors.

Lizzi Hawkins

Winter one-night stand

The clouds shed their winter skins;
turned February blank.
Building a body, a great white woman
whose hips were hills, whose cheeks could not flush rose.
Though, tightly, she grasped him, the moor.

A glint in the crag's eye and the curlews cried love
of the bodies locked in gravity's embrace.
At night, the sky sparked back where their palms met.
The verse of her wrists was a psalm
across the valley's nape.

Where her fingertips capped the trees
the wood sang out tremors of frost;
it had begun to ache with ice,
and he, her counterpart
was harshened, taut.

Under her lovely flesh,
snow flexed its hold
on rivers, soil.
Roots balled like fists upheld.
The gentle body was a battlefield of cold.

When dawn sun-tipped the pine sills,
the hills wept her pale passing.
But the crows, hung above
the sapping body on the grass, brayed:

> Such things as these don't last.
> Such things as these cannot bring life.

Lizzi Hawkins

Winter-thief

The cold snatched breath from our mouths
and wrung it out dry. Hard coils of air
anchored at our lips,
leaving us tongue-tied;
our trusts unshared.

The sky bucked, folded white
so that frost crystallised a snap-shot
of our words, cutting
their syllables short:
their cropped, curt places bearing chill.

The snowflakes caught on my eyelashes,
so when I looked at you I was snow-blind;
your face furred white
like an unmade decision –
unclear, like a promise unpicked.

Clouds crumpled at the blanched brows
of hills. The distance in your voice
exceeded your body, like it was rising over those hills;
counter weighting the closeness
of you.

As you walked away,
your footprints disappeared in the snow,
like the warmth of your palm on my palm,
or the birds dissolving their dark freight from the trees.
Disturbed by the cold.

MATTHEW HEDLEY STOPPARD

Leather Was Thrown

1.

David watched himself throw jabs and uppercuts in the dressing room mirror. He continued to slash at the air in front of him until his tightly bandaged hands blurred to white smudges. Stopping to examine himself, he faced the mirror: sweat trembled on the end of his flat nose, his polyester vest shimmered, and his dented cheeks reddened. He then turned to leer at his muscular back noticing its resemblance to an elephant's head.

2.

The main hall of the North Wingfield W.M.C. was swollen with people. Tables were perpendicularly situated, like a mosaic, around the boxing ring in the centre. The air was grey and blue with smoke and bad language. All conversation conflated to a slow growl, occasionally disrupted by a phlegm-coated cackle.

Behind the bar, the Landlord rallied his staff, as the queue of drinkers was three-deep. The flabby triceps of the thirty-something barmaid tightened at each pull of the cask pump-handle; froth spat from the nozzle into a dimpled beer-mug. She looked to the bald barman confusedly selecting a straight pint glass and filling it with a bitter soufflé produced from badly poured lager. The Landlord leaned on the cash register for a moment and pinched his cigarette and took a delicate sip of Mild from a pudgy half-pint glass. The queue finally thinned out.

Piss pierced the urinal cakes in the Gent's toilets. and a septuagenarian with walking sticks struggled to vacate a cubicle. In the Ladies' toilets, perms were primped and knickers were dropped around ankles and toilet paper was exchanged underneath the partitions of the cubicles.

To the right of the Ladies' toilet entrance, at the front of the hall, was a shoulder-high stage exhibiting a pile of raffle prizes and trophies depicting faux-gold boxing figures. Cheap boxes of chocolates leaned against giant bottles of whiskey and a basket of toiletries and bath salts propped up a giant beribboned teddy bear. A microphone stand and stained bucket, filled with raffle tickets, stood a yard, stage-left, from the array of tawdry awards allocated for tonight's competitors.

3.

Blood thumped up and down David's teenage limbs as he hopped from right to left, all the while fixing his stare on the reflection in the dressing room mirror. His momentum slowed to a side-to-side sway on the balls of his feet. He ceased moving. Placing his palms either side of the pearl necklace of light bulbs around the mirror he leaned forward to rest his face on the glass. David could feel the sharp chill on his cheek, neck and earlobe until the temperature changed to a clean warmth; he gazed through a stool in the corner, and through what ever was behind it. He was overwhelmed with memory.

Gerry burst into the dressing room with a net bag of boxing equipment. DANESMOOR AMATEUR BOXING CLUB was stitched into the back of the tracksuit jacket he was wearing and a chunky gold chain bounced off his polo-shirt collar as he waddled towards David. Gerry, trainer and cutman, was old and heavy-set but his movements had snap and purpose. He slammed the net bag down and wrested David from the mirror.

They stood toe-to-toe. Gerry clasped David's beading head between his palms and thumbed Vaseline across his eyebrows to prevent sweat stinging the eyes. Kneeling down, he dropped to David's boots to ensure the laces were tied tight underneath his kneecap. He stood up and noticed an adrift pair of eyes. Gerry lightly slapped the lad across the face in demand of his attention. He then reached into the net bag and pulled out a pair of cherry-coloured boxing gloves; they were bulbous, the leather had bubbled and started to peel. Gerry held the gloves open and David rammed his fists into them, the laces were wrapped around his wrist securely and tied in a double-knot.

After more rummaging in his net bag, Gerry retrieved a pair of focus pads. He held them up in front of his face at eye-level, showing the white-circled targets on the flat sides. A fighting stance was assumed: David arranged his footwork and picked his fists up to his chin, his left jabbing hand hovering in anticipation of striking the corresponding pad. His right was held close to his cheekbone for protection from counterpunches.

Gerry nodded and David jabbed fiercely, conserving his right fist. He jabbed without restraint, and then released his right fist, all his shoulder committed to the punch. The air sewn into the foam pad wheezed through the cross-stitching. Each attack was swift, tearing forth and quickly returning to cover his face. David emitted an 'nst, nst' sound with each jab and a gasp when launching a haymaker.

He stopped. Gerry changed the position of the pads to a lower height so they were facing each other across his chest. David's back curled and he began a rhythmic attack of left and right hooks.

Finally uppercuts. Gerry kept the pads at chest-height but turned them to face the floor. David looked to the floor too and began to pound upwards. He felt the sting of lactic acid building in his back and shoulders and a warm ache in his elbows and biceps. His last uppercut was feral and inaccurate, missing the target, catching the underside of pad, ripping it from Gerry's hand. David stood up straight to see Gerry scowling at him wearing only one focus pad.

The focus pads were gathered and Gerry produced a gaudy dressing gown with gaping sleeves. The same logo on his tracksuit jacket was sewn onto the back of it, except there was the addition of DAVID TOPLISS underneath. He carefully helped David into the gown. The belt was not tied and it billowed like a washing-line-hung sheet in the wind when he moved.

A chunky red head guard was placed on David, cross-laced, and knotted. There were holes for his ears and his catlicked hair spiked out of the top. The tight fit of the head guard pushed his cheeks towards his nose and his brow into his eye sockets.

As the cheap material of the dressing gown and enclosure of the head guard quickened David's sweating, Gerry pulled a gum shield from his trouser pocket, blew off specks of fluff and tobacco, and stuffed it into David's mouth. He chewed until it slid into the jags of his teeth.

'Uh yuh ready, lad?' Gerry asked.

David replied: 'Umgrf.'

4.

The tipsy assembly ignored the prelude match of two twelve year-olds scrapping in the ring; their ill-fitting uniforms drowned them in polyester; their training failed them. They fought like rag-dolls, floppy and loose-limbed. At ringside, two judges sat at a cleared buffet table and scribbled on clipboards in front of them. Pints lined up on the apron wobbled when one of the young pugilists stomped the canvas in a moment of mistimed footwork.

Two men, one table back from the boxing ring, chatted with drinks held at chest height:

'Toppo comin' tuh watch David fight tonate?'

'Don't reckon so. 'E wohrrin Elm Tree at half eleven this mornin' and 'e woh tryin' tuh sell a fishin' rod tuh pay forra ticket to come tonate.

'So, 'e left theah 'bout three-ish an' carried on tuh Red Lion wih 'is fishin' rod. 'E has another four pints in theah an' Neville Cartwright walks in. Toppo knew that Nev was a keen angler and went down tuh Holmegate pond at least twice a week. Toppo, three-parts-pissed, starts eggin' Nev to buy this rod an' Nev's 'avin' none of it. They gerrinn a tussle an' Toppo falls face-first intuh' disco speaker at end oh bar and bust 'is cheek open... Jacko, behine bar, picked 'im up and chucked 'im tuh kerb.

'After that, he woh seen in Three Horse Shoes toilets wadding' gash on his face wih toilet paper. Apparently he looked a right state! No one's seen 'im since.

'Thing is: if 'e hadn't of spent 'is money on ale this afternoon, he would've 'ad enough to buy a ticket to come watch David tonate.'

The third, and final, round started. The spectators rose, in a soused Mexican wave, and barked at the twelve year-olds fight for two crucial minutes. Cries of 'Goowan!' and 'Use yuh jab!' scratched through the air. Head guards clashed and bounced and swinging boxing gloves slapped against arms and shoulder blades. The two men one table back from the boxing ring stood unfazed by the bloodlust:

'Is Toppo comin' then or what?'

5.

David and Gerry were exiting the dressing room when a twelve year-old pugilist, wearing a 'Runner-up' medal, came hurtling towards the door. He tore through the middle of them; chin on chest, head down, and his arms swinging uncontrollably, because of the oversized boxing gloves laced around his wrists.

He scrambled to the stool in the corner and sat down. His eyes bulged with water as he looked down at the laces on his gloves. Fumbling at the double-knots with gloved fingers, he shook and became weak. The heat from crying made his face look raw and tears trickled to his jaw-line, rheumy bubbles on his lips.

Realising he couldn't untie the glove laces, he gnawed at them ferociously. They didn't loosen and he could taste his mucus, which had soaked into the strings as he was biting them. He looked up, inhaled and let out throaty wheeze. Hunched over and shuddering with sobbing hiccups, he wept into the palms of his boxing gloves.

6.

Water evacuated the coffin-sized cistern above the urinal and spluttered through the nozzles of the flushing system. A stiff limbed man zipped his trouserflies and passed through the swinging door to the main hall. Diluted drain urine babbled in the empty Gent's.

A foot slipped through the narrow window above the sinks, then a white-socked ankle, followed by a denim leg. The foot searched for a platform. A grunt and cough came from outside the window. The foot found the sink and the rest of Toppo's body awkwardly slipped through; he caught the back of his jacket on a latch and it came up over his head until it ripped free.

Toppo scanned the room – there wasn't a mirror in the Gent's. He bent over and looked at the funhouse reflection of his face in the tap handles on the sink: the gash on his face was stuccoed with blood-soaked toilet paper that had dried. Toppo's right middle and index fingers dug in behind the toilet paper and scraped down, peeling away to reveal a bloody flap of skin that looked like a fish's gill. He sucked his teeth at the pain and the sight of his wound and scuttled into the end cubicle to re-wad it and wipe away the blood.

With new makeshift dressing on his face, Toppo returned to the tap handle and smoothed his hair until he was pleased with its sleekness. Trying to disguise his drunkenness, he walked in an overly conservative manner to the Gent's door and casually stepped out into the main hall to see David hop onto the boxing ring apron.

7.

'Erm, Thank you!' The rumble of conversation was silenced as the Landlord stood beside the trophies and prizes on the stage in the main hall. He blew into the microphone to gauge the volume and continued: 'We 'ave reached tonigh's main event.' He pronounced each word as precisely as he knew best. 'The final match between the Chaddeston Youths' Gym and Danesmoor Amateur Boxing Club is between Carl Baines, from Derby, and David Topliss, from Danesmoor. This is a match of three two-minute rounds. It will be scored by Judges Mark Kenny and Aubrey Sharratt. Referee is Cliff 'Pops' Wilson. And the raffle for the big teddy will be drawn afterwards.' Applause roared and microphone feedback screeched; the crowd turned to the boxing ring.

David stepped through the ropes, his dressing gown wafting behind him. He tried to hop on the balls of his feet only to find his head hitting the polystyrene tiles of the ceiling – the base of the ring was too large for the height of the hall.

Gerry stood next to Lee in David's corner leaning on the taut ropes attached to the corner post, holding a bucket of water and sponge. Lee, co-owner of the boxing club, stood tall with his hands clamped around the middle rope. He was approaching thirty yet his bespectacled face looked both wise and concerned. David strode over to his corner and Gerry handed the bucket to Lee so he could disrobe David. Gerry patted David's face with globules of Vaseline and squeezed the sponge over his head. The cold water from the sponge crept between the gaps of the head guard, behind David's ears. He turned to evaluate his opponent: he was meatier; his arms were plump, almost doughy, compared to the prone sinew of David's. The opponent was swarthy, dark skin-types tended not to show bruises during fights, but David's skin was wan and large shadowy bruises appeared on him even during sparring.

8.

Round One: The bell pinged and David pounced from his corner. His back defensively hunched, jabbing hand poised, right hand covered his face, and elbows tucked into his ribs. They circled the ring looking for openings to release a jab. Bobbing like a moored ship, David's opponent looked sluggish and in no manner possessed the same agility.

David skidded on his tiptoes into his opponent and unleashed snapped jabs; they slapped against shielding boxing gloves and clattered on the head guard. Sharply, he pushed his shoulder into a rolling right-hook connecting with ribs. With his opponent winded, David's jabs stung his lip only to be blocked by gloves again.

A minute had passed and Toppo came spilling through the crowd, veering off table edges and inconsiderately bumping shoulders with onlookers. He stumbled to the ring apron: 'Goowan, son! Goowan, David-lad! Pagger 'im!' David's fists dropped and he looked to where his father was. His opponent capitalised on the distraction and landed an overhand punch where the head guard exposed the face. Low groans swept across the crowd and David tumbled backwards, his head brushing the ceiling. 'Pick yuh fists up, David-lad! Yer half-hearted!' David was adrift; his head tilted wistfully to one side and he was unable to bring his fists up to his chin. Stalking forward, the opponent wound up another haymaker. The bell pinged again.

Slipping through the ropes Lee guided David to his corner and Gerry passed a stool to them. Once David was seated, Gerry reached round and pulled his gum shield out and squeezed the soaked sponge over his head, into his mouth. 'That round woh yourn, David,' Lee said leaning low to David's face. He pointed his finger at the bruised eye before him. 'But yuh got tuh keep that jab up and keep that right hand over yuh face 'cos he'll want pick on it. You guh out and win this roun' an' wih can relax in t'third.' Lee clutched David's wrists and held his fists up: 'Keep 'em up and keep 'im guessin'. You're faster. Land them jabs and get points.' Gerry stuffed the gum shield back in and smeared Vaseline across David's face. The bell pinged.

'Wadya say to 'im, Lee!' Toppo continued to snarl: 'Lee! Lee! Yeah, thought so. Nothin'. Lee! Lee!' David plodded out of the corner, his hands dangled at his sides. Without hesitation his opponent came out too and slammed a right-hook in his midriff. David was bent double. He was sat cross-legged on the hearth rug in front of the gas fire – one bar glowing. Pigeon coos echoed down the chimney; toes wriggled in the carpet at the edge of the rug. Hurtful, growling words whirred through the kitchen door, adjoining the living room, followed by shrill pleads. Men dressed as bears sang nursery rhymes and danced on the television screen. David ate chocolate breakfast cereal facing the floor, an overhand rabbit-punch cracked him on the back of the head. The dunt deafened him and excited the crowd. The boards below the boxing ring canvas jerked under the indecisive steps of the referee, who stepped into examine the legitimacy of the fight. David's thunderstruck face looked up. The fracas in the kitchen intensified as David toddled towards it. Two slaps resonated quickly followed by cutlery clattering and finally a single hollow wallop against sheet metal. David tugged on the door handle and leant back; the latch came free to reveal the scene in the kitchen and he could see his opponent's thigh-sized arm winding up to deliver another haymaker. Before recognising its release, the punch slammed into David's face and he felt his eye puncture and his knees buckle. David saw his mother, facedown, on the floor with her arm bent backwards into the washing machine drum and her head resting against its front panel. His father stood with his fists clenched, scowling at the woman on the floor attempting to stand up, one-handedly, only to fall on her face again. 'Gerrup! Gerrup!' Toppo raged by the ringside. 'Yer not gonna lehmme down, lad' David supine on the canvas, a mackerel-coloured bruise across his nose and eye. The referee signalled a knockout and held up the victor's glove.

Toppo clawed at the ropes and scrambled into the ring. He made a beeline for the black and white striped shirt. Arms flailing, Toppo struck the referee as well as the young boxer next him. The Chaddeston coaching staff bundled into the ring to restrain Toppo; so did Gerry and Lee. Members of the crowd cheered as they watched the melee in the ring thrash, and obliviously trample David.

9.

Outside in the car park, in the back of a hatchback, a boy wearing a runner-up medal sat sucking pop through a straw. His father, in the front, curled round, draped his arm over the headrest, to face his son: 'Do you want have a go at football instead?'

SARAH BROOKS

Instructions in Italian

Drink down your coffee in one.
Take it black and sweet.

Observe the play of sun on skin,
the way heat slows your blood,
the way pupils contract
in unaccustomed light.

Read the signs
lizards leave
in dust.

The stirring earth cracks the paving stones
in the piazza.
Offer sweat from your skin to appease it.

Walk past the men who sit outside cafés,
their figures curved
to the contours of crumbling walls.
If they offer you a cigarette,
don't take it.

Watch the sea
from a distance.
Don't trust the water
when it can't be distinguished from sky.

Find your bearings
by the island and its crooked tree.

Breathe in sand,
count each grain in your seashore lungs.
Listen to the waves in the conch of your ear.

Eat bread the widow next door bakes for you.
Lick salt from your lips.
Buy your fish
from the women in the market on Saturdays,
who have scales for fingernails
and the flicker of fins in their hair.

SARAH BROOKS

Santa Trinita, Florence

For a euro you can buy two minutes' light
to illuminate the chapel in the corner,
where a child falls from a window,
just down the road from here,
by the looks of it,
and you can't help
but bring murder to mind
- where were his parents?
Who stands in the shadows
in the street outside, speaking
of what new marvels?
What did the angel see?

Wondrous, the city
in these strange days
of men who magic science into art.

Let time tread on its own toes.
Wake the saints who
jetlagged, step into an unfamiliar century
just in time to resurrect the dead,
before the lights go out.

Aissa Gallie

Film Piece: The Spaces Between Us

Meanwood Park: two children are playing a game of catch with their mother. The scene is silent except for the sound of the wind that would be rushing past their ears. As she runs after them, just missing them as she reaches out to 'tig', the mother's breath can be heard. The children's laughter fades in as they run in opposite directions until they are equidistant from mum who stands in the middle. They turn to her and laugh. She looks at one and then the other, she too laughs, breathlessly. Then she sits down where she is. Simultaneously the two children run towards her and pile on top.

The camera pans up and looks down at a bird's eye view of the three. They are all touching. Then as they slowly separate there is a moment of symmetry in their movement, each individual mirroring the other. The scene is frozen. The bodies form a frame around a small hexagonal space in between them. The camera zooms in onto the space until it pixelates. The zoom moves further in on the pixilation's and reveals that the picture of this space is made up of hundreds of pictures of this space, repeated over and over. A kaleidoscopic turning of the screen allows these pictures to play and fall within each other, every turn revealing a new form, made up of the same pictures. An Escher-like fractal is formed from the pictures of the space. The scene is frozen. The camera zooms out until a singular picture of this framed space fills the screen again. As the mother and her children move apart, the frame is broken, yet a trace remains. Real time returns with real sound.

MAX DUNBAR

A Little Legal Difficulty

The final refrain from some Gary Barlow song was in Will's head. Robin had been singing it since New Year's Eve.

'Hopin' to find a man that *knows* me...' He swivelled a little on the sofa, and pointed his index finger in a *bdm*-tish style. 'That man is *me*...'

'What is it with you and that song?'

'I always thought that if men menstruated,' Robin said, 'then Gary Barlow would provide that song to the advert for male tampons. Like the Manidom.'

'I can see it. I can see it.' Getting into the joke. 'Like there would be a shot of a guy playing football in the park, he scores a goal, his mates are all around, tousling his hair, lifting him up –'

'And that's the freeze frame. His hair's all tousled –'

'That's it. Freeze, and then – *that man is me...*'

They cracked up, even Little Jay, sat between them, the only girl in the room, she was laughing along at the perplexity of it all. Then Big Jay came in and announced that suppertime was ready.

It was the first weekend since NYE and they planned to fill up on pasta bake before heading out to Resolution. That was something Will loved about his scene in Hyde Park. Most students lived on class A's and ready meals. But Will and his friends could cook. Big Jay even talked of getting an allotment together, when the weather turned.

She sat now, having served, the room low in its warmth

and darkness, candles glimmering distorted in the Shiraz bottles, the Afghan rug and Viva Palestina posters reduced to vague shapes, the wind pitching up, up, up. Big Jay sat with the trembling expectation of the good host who wonders if she's good enough.

Will's voice was muffled by bows and tomato. 'Good stuff, Jay. Amazing.'

Robin pulled a clove of garlic from between his front molars. 'Will – we aren't on the pull tonight, are we?'

'Resolution? I doubt it.'

Little Jay was next to Will and she punched his arm. Little Jay did that a lot. 'Hey Will – what about *la fila Brasilia*?'

'*La fila Brasilia* – I haven't seen her for a coupla weeks now.'

'*Everyone* was all over that,' Robin said. 'At the Drydock. She loved you, Will.'

'Well, we were meant to go for a coffee; didn't. Not the end of the world.'

'She wanted to get *fisted*.'

'Don't be uncouth, dear.'

'*Fisted*,' Robin said. There was a strange discordancy to his voice, almost musical but not quite, and it grated when he was amused. '*Fisted*, until your hand came out of her throat and waved.' Robin demonstrated as best he could.

Big Jay was looking at him. Big Jay the nurturer and protector. 'How's the single life treating you?'

'Too early to say,' Will replied. His relationship with Suzy from York had dissolved that autumn in a spirit of goodwill; he still saw her at Sandinistas and the Drydock. He spoke truthfully, it really was too early to say. Could do with boning something, though. Wouldn't be too long. He had faith. People told him he looked like a slimmer Guy Garvey.

Little Jay and Will did all the washing up; Will insisted on this, because they were the two guests; Robin and Big Jay lived in the rooms upstairs.

A flick of foam on his cheek and he turned, Little Jay laughing again, then recoiling back. 'God, you have eaten too much garlic. My eyes! My beautiful eyes!'

'Well,' he said, mock-pedantic, 'I smell of garlic on this one occasion, but you happen to smell of fish *all the time*, and not even *good* fish – like, *marlin*, or some shit.'

'I don't care.' She folded her arms, doing her Violet Elizabeth Bott. 'The scent of fish has been known to be very powerful in attracting –'

'Other fish.'

'Yep. Fish come to me, mistaking me for one of their own, and then I eat them.' She did a minature jig. Then, in her *Spaceghost* voice: 'Now the dance is a dance of sadness.'

She flicked him again. He flicked her back – put both hands in the suds, hauled out as much as he could and upended it onto her happy, astonished face. Covered in foam. Enduring image. Like on New Year's Day when he'd been out picking up snow in buckets so they could have water and the wet blow to the back of his head, he had turned around and she'd been on the fucking roof, had scraped her weapon off the guttering, laughing triumph in her starfish hat and foul-weather jacket.

When the water fight ended Will was soaked top to tail and laughing like hell and full of the combative passion that their little wrestling matches always gave him. They had barely made a start on the washing up, and then came a knock on the door.

Little Jay, also drenched: 'I hope that's Gallo. I could do with a line.' She vanished, and came back skipping. 'Gallo! Gallo is here!'

Gallo was doing the same degree as Will: always coked up, flamboyantly neoconservative, he could make eating soup look decadent. He shook Will's hand and began racking up on the *Lost Horizons* CD case. 'Happy new year, mate. Have a good one?'

'Craziness. Carnage.' He began the story, but Little Jay kept interrupting, and caught Gallo's attention; she ended up finishing the tale.

Rather than the usual end of year houseparty they had gone to a little pub up in Horton-on-Ribblesdale. It had been a guaranteed lockin; what they hadn't expected was that the lockin would last three days. This was the worst cold snap in three decades, and the Yorkshire highlands were hit hard. They were snowed in from two am on New Year's Day, and it became a survivalist scene that reminded Will of Glasto and Reading and his year in the Far East: cooking communal meals and washing up with melted snow. What he remembered most about that time was the snowball fight Little Jay had started, the way it rippled out until even the landlord and bar staff were throwing snowballs and laughing.

'The landlord was totally fine. We ran out of class As on around the second day, but this guy had a dope stash.'

'Good skills, man.' He offered the case Jay's way.

Later, after Resolution, in another house, near the Elsix Social, in a room with three close friends, snowing outside, nothing mattering, the pulling thing or anything, Gallo holding court: ' – and this Fairfax guy was saying, you know, graduating this year, you have no idea what's gonna hit you, no idea whatsoever. The worst time to graduate since the thirties.'

'I don't know. Students have more disposable income than ever before.'

'Exactly!' He clipped at the powder with his MasterCard. 'We'll miss it. *Out there is chaos.*'

'As long as I'm not still here in five years, walking into

the Social in bare feet on a Sunday morning,' Will said. The room erupted. They all knew who he was talking about.

'Driving a bus, singing Alisha's Attic,' Robin cackled. He extended his arms, then pulled them up and down as if manipulating a steering wheel. '*I am, I feel ... I sometimes think that you forget...*'

'Well, you'll be alright,' Robin said. 'Teaching's a solid profession.'

Gallo: 'Yeah. You're Mr Hyde Park!'

Will laughed. 'Who's Miss Hyde Park?'

'*I'm* Miss Hyde Park!' Little Jay cried. 'I could get up at one of those beauty contests, take some pills – and dance!'

She got up and danced around the room; it had been a long night, but she showed no signs of flagging. There was perfect and thoughtless co-ordination in her tiny frame. She high-kicked, but Gallo made no move to protect the DVD case. They had been at the club four hours and Little Jay had danced on podium pretty much all that time. Flirting with loads of guys but never taking one home; Little Jay didn't seem to want much of anything.

'So when are we doing the nine at nine?'

'The nine at nine,' Will said, 'will be at mine. Wednesday.' He took the DVD case.

'Wednesday?'

'Yep.' Fired back a line.

'Good.'

'Carlo? Isn't he the one who's always going on about Iraq?'

'Iran,' Gallo corrected. 'Always going on about *Iran*. About revolution in Iran, the democratisation of the Muslim world, he's on this big Richard Dawkins thing.'

Little Jay was still dancing, and singing now, sweet and low. 'If I am not for myself,' she sang, 'who will be for me?'

'Have you *read* that book?' Will spoke up. 'It's just a fucking religious rant. The Islamic Republic is a *mature democracy*, and Western liberals should just stop hoping for a velvet revolution and thinking that the average Iranian is represented by these well-heeled exiles who haven't even lived in the country for decades.'

'If not now, when?' Little Jay sang, and pirouetted into the corridor.

'Anyway, what happened to *la fila Brasilia*?' Gallo asked. 'Is she still seeing Paulo?'

'He fisted it,' Robin laughed.

'No, Paulo's not been around for a while,' Will said. 'He basically had a breakdown. Too much mescaline. He was at this party and this psychology student was trying to section him. In the end he was lying in Brudenell Road with this girl trying to convince him that he *was* real, he *wasn't* going to dissolve, he *was* Paulo. I heard that he moved to Texas with his dad. He's looking after buffalos now.'

'Shit, where's Little Jay?'

'Is that the plural?'

'Will, go and check on Little Jay,' Gallo said.

'She'll be fine. You know what she's like, she's a total maniac but she never really goes under.'

Headrush when he stood up. 'I'll go.'

'Tending a herd of *buffali*.'

The bathroom was wide open and Little Jay leant on the sink, writing something in the child's exercise pad she always carried with her. It had a friendly one-eyed monster on the cover.

'Are you okay?' Will closed the door. 'They sent me here to check on you.'

'Fine. Went in here to have a piss and then got thinking about things. Couldn't piss, man, it's this coke.'

'I know a cure for that.'

'Yeah?'

'Absolutely,' Will said, and kissed her lips. He knew he

was a good kisser and Jay's resistance didn't kick in for a few seconds. Then she pulled away. 'Thanks, mate, I appreciate this –'

'Oh, this is just the warm-up,' he said, and punched her in the stomach. Her wind went and he knocked her to the ground. Little Jay was strong as well as little, but at six foot one and ten stone, Will had a clear physical advantage. Pinned her to the floor, right hand on her neck, and then used his left hand to unclip her rhinestone belt and lever the jeans down enough to achieve entry. Her kicks and struggles made it better. Lust, he thought, is cold and comes like ice in the chest.

Drugs had never inhibited his sexual prowess, and he was hard as soon as he was near her. She cried out in definite pain, but he doubted anyone would hear over Big Jay's boyfriend's set.

He left her undone and sobbing on the bathroom floor and shut the door and hit the bedroom. Suzy from York had come up for a line with one of her mates. They exchanged smiles.

'How is she?' Gallo asked.

'Fine. She had trouble pissing.'

'I know a cure for that,' Robin laughed.

'Yeah, so you had to bone her for a bit,' Suzy said.

'Oh yeah. Relax those uteral walls.'

'I think not. One pill and you're button mushroom city, babe.'

'Does your sister tell you *everything*?'

'Aren't you hating the weather?' Suzy asked. 'Everyone's talking about it.'

'Like, it's always been a signifier of a dull personality that you talk about the weather,' Gallo was racking up again, 'but now *everyone's talking about the weather!* The papers are just like: IT'S FUCKING SNOWING!'

'The media is just like snow and lists and the fucking

Chilcott inquiry,' Will said. 'How many times do we have to go through this before it's established that this was an *illegal fucking war*?'

'Is the plural of cacti "cacti"?'

Ten days until the beginning of term and Will tried to get as much uni work as possible done during the day. Christmas was a dull time, bar the usual timewarp reunion the night before, and he'd been determined to fill it. His dissertation was a comparative study of Karen Armstrong and Terry Eagleton. Difficult to start work in the morning, but he had fun once he got into it, and afterwards there was a happy exhaustion like the way he felt after playing football. He lost a day when they did the nine at nine (he and eight other men watched the entire *Lord of the Rings* trilogy from nine o'clock onwards) and anyway things always fell apart around six, when they started thinking about cooking, and people would drop round, and wine would be poured and joints lit and discussions held about whether to put the Eddie Murphy DVD on or watch *Touching the Void* or maybe have a pint down the Royal Park or maybe even the Social?

As it happened Thursday afternoon they were in the Royal Park, a student barn that had nothing going for it except proximity. Big Jay asked: 'Has anyone seen Little Jay?'

'Little Jay is *lame*,' said Gallo. 'I'm barred from here, I came here specifically to give her the Primo Levi book back, and she's not here.'

'You know what she's like,' Robin said. 'She'll go out, get *pissed as a bastard*, do loads of drugs for a few days and then she'll just lock herself in her room with a case of wine, doing uni work. Remember that afternoon drink, Evil Ray's birthday, when we were at the dogs? She was wrecked but that night she went home and did three thousand on the fallacy of postmodernism or whatever. Got a sixty-one, man.'

'Yeah but she's not even responding through Facebook.' Big Jay the nurturer and protector.

'On Twitter.'

'In Jay's honour,' Gallo said, 'we should rename Twitter to 'Flailer'.'

'Forget about Little Jay. Think of Gallo.' Gallo had been barred from the Royal Park for shagging a fresher in the toilets. 'He's here with the Primo Levi book, running the gauntlet for Little Jay, and she's not here!'

'I'll text her again.' Big Jay concentrated over her mobile like someone defusing a bomb. Then she burst out laughing. 'Hey Gallo – your name on predictive text comes out as 'thong'.'

At the bar Will got talking to a girl from Windsor that he vaguely recognised from the Beetle's seminar.

'Legoland,' Will said. 'Bet everyone says that.'

'Yeah. Legoland. I don't care, man. I'm proud of Legoland.'

'You should be. Hey, I always wondered. When you visit Legoland, are the Lego houses like to scale – you know, with a Lego house the size of an actual house, but made of –'

'They *are* to scale,' the girl confirmed, 'but they're not made of Lego. I mean, you couldn't build an actual Lego house that people could live in – there would be structural issues.'

'Right, health and safety –'

'Yeah. They're painted to look like Lego but it's actually wood.'

'A magical illusion shattered.'

'That summer I learned a lot.'

They arranged to head back to her place on Kensington Terrace where a small party was taking place. Will went back to the table to get his Berghaus jacket. Robin was slumped back against the wood with his eyes closed. 'Ha, can tell who can't handle afternoon drinking!' Will ruffled his hair.

'That man is *me*...'

' – and we ended up at this place in Chapel Allerton with loads of guys just completely monged out on ketamine, with one or two cyber kids going in and out – just blundered in, pissed as a *bastard*...'

'Like Crasher kids!'

'Yeah, like Crasher kids, I felt like I died and woke up in fucking 2002.'

'Chapel Allerton, man. They got the West Indian Centre, but apart from that it's just fucking grim. Grim and *wrong*.'

'Like the *essence*. The *essence* of wrong.'

He had run into his housemates at the Kensington Terrace bash. They were humanities students on the wilder orbits of his circle. There was a guy in a flat cap spinning sci trance from behind a set of decks, a woman with shaved hair struggling into a fireman's uniform, some guy dressed as Lana Croft, Will was skinning up a joint and thinking of how Brudenell had looked as they trekked up there against furious elements, and he had raised his face to see a typhoon of snowflakes rocket past the old Jackson's and the hardware shop and down the road towards him, the wind matching the curve and twist of the street with an eerie exactitude. He hadn't seen the Legoland girl recently.

The back garden had a decent sized shed. You saw the huddled lights of congregation. A grey cat skirted across the roof. He dashed through a curtain of snowfall and lit his joint. Gallo was there. So was the Lego girl.

His reefer went round. Conversation went, but he couldn't follow it. Then he was in the Lego girl's bedroom. Alone with her. Scented candles. There was some kind of ambient music on her Spotify, Groove Armada or possibly Clubbed Out, he wasn't too sure, and evidently he'd pulled without really trying.

'Bet you weren't expecting me to kiss you,' she breathed

in his face. Weird mint surface to her breath.

'Actually I was.' He stroked the curve of her neck, loving the resistance of its fuzz. 'My pheromones told me that you were attracted to me, it was just a matter of time.'

'Pheremone – isn't that the stuff they have in the SU vending machines, in the male bogs? Guys smear it on at traffic light parties?'

'Must have been one hell of a traffic light party.' Hand massaging the breast. 'If you ended up in the lads' bogs.'

Laughed breath in his ear. 'I had traffic light *orgies*. Pure traffic love action. Hey, I was in that gay bar in Call Lane, and they had a vending machine that sold *anal beads*.'

Monday and sorting out the timetable for the semester ahead. He walked up to the Terrace early afternoon. The snow was churned to slush and the sun was out for the first time in weeks.

He was walking with Gallo. In the foyer of the SU they saw Little Jay, on her way out. Gallo hailed her and she jumped. Girl looked like shit, Will thought; sweaty green combats, that old fleece she wore in bed, roots creeping through the dye.

Little Jay turned to Gallo. She clocked Will and their eyes met. She walked around him as if he was a burning bin. Gallo wheeled on one foot, yelled out in concern, but Little Jay's footsteps quickened and then receded. Will didn't even turn round.

'Fuck's all that about?' Gallo asked.

'Christ knows. Women.'

'Strange fish. Yep.'

They got a couple of pints and found Robin on a table with Evil Ray, Ben, Suzy, Vanessa and some others. Beers and packets of subsidised food.

'Hey hey!' Robin yelled. 'How was that Lego slut? I believe you spent the whole weekend with her.'

'That's at my discretion.' Will folded his arms in a silence that boosted his credibility as no words could.

'So what's the deal?' Big Jay asked. 'Is she like *made* of Lego?'

'Yes. That's exactly right. She is physically *made* of Lego.'

'It's just a question of fitting the bricks together,' Gallo advised. 'Sometimes you can make a house. Sometimes you can make an airport. And Robin, don't ask questions. You never fucking *talk* about the woman you fuck –'

'Best part. That's what the Italians say. Anyway, I talk about the bird I pulled at the West Indian Centre.'

Will said: 'Doesn't your chatup technique consist simply of going up to women at random and saying that you have '*quite* the cock'?'

'I don't know *why*,' Gallo said. 'She wasn't Lego, man. This girl was *Duplo*.'

'Don't matter,' Robin said. 'Just means there's more to love.'

'Please! There's ladies present.'

'Technically,' Will added. 'And aren't you a virgin, Gallo?'

'I'm like the Jonas Brothers. I'm saving myself for Jesus.'

'I don't give a fuck, because women talk about men in *exactly* the way that men talk about women,' Robin insisted. 'And women want to be dominated as much as men want to dominate. Case in point: Big Jay. She comes across all sweet and cuddly but she *loves* the cock. I was in the room next to hers all through second year and you just *did not sleep* when her boyfriend was round.'

By this time the girls were throwing pizza crust and condiment packets at him. 'They love it, those Lego whores!' Robin cried out. 'Fucking sticklebrick sluts! Jesus, that's fucking *mustard* on my face.'

'And not even good mustard. French mustard.'

'Freedom mustard,' Will said. 'They renamed it in 2003.'

First week of lectures. Two hours to kill until constitutional theory and he was having a coffee and a cram with Lorna the Lego girl. She was bitching about the PhD student taking the course.

' – and he's just so fucking narrow minded, he won't let you cite anything from queer theory or deconstructionism, you can't cite Chomsky because he said something nice about Pol Pot in the 1970s, you can't talk about Ed Herman because –'

'Because of Srebrenica. Because of what he said about what supposedly happened in the Balkans in the mid fucking nineties.'

'Exactly. Six degrees of separation. You can't cite Finkelstein because he was in Palestine negotiating with Hamas.'

'He had a latte with David Irving.'

'He got stuck in a lift with Robert Faurisson in 1998.'

'Exactly.'

Big Jay and her boyfriend sat down. 'Sorry, do you mind? –'

'No, no, you're good –'

Clatter and scrape of chairs. Big Jay's boyfriend got out a little ten-inch Dell. 'Right, this better work,' he muttered. 'If I don't get on to Google books in the next twenty minutes I am gonna physically get rimmed up the arse.'

'Hey, you're too polite,' Lorna said. 'It's like when you're about to pass someone in the corridor, and you do that pathetic little dance, and you're trying to make space for them to pass you while they're trying to do the same –'

'Fucking wifi, why does the wifi in this building never work.'

'Babe, you need to put the key in.'

'I *am* entering the key. I've entered it like *nine* times.'

'Nine times?' Will asked. 'Literally *nine* times?'

'I am a computer,' Big Jay's boyfriend said in a robot

voice. 'I only do what you tell me.'

Vibrato of a phone. Big Jay picked up and started talking.

' – I *am* telling you to do it, *grrrrrrrr*... but you're not telling me *properly*...'

Big Jay lowered her voice and walked away from the table. The SU cafe was a thoroughfare this time of day and she had to raise her voice, a hand cupped over one ear. Will felt a prickle of insecurity. Maybe Lorna would be offended by the robot voice. Maybe it would remind her of Stephen Hawking. Her brother was in a wheelchair.

'*Cocking* computer!' Big Jay's boyfriend yelled.

Gallo appeared from somewhere. 'What's the story, Bala-fucking-mory. Hey, tell you about this twat in my seminar. He was like: *I drove into Chester city centre yesterday and found to my horror that it had been pedestrianised!*'

'Like, he *was* Alan Partridge?'

'He *was* Alan Partridge.'

'I mean does Chester even *have* a city centre anyway? Or is there just like a fire in a tin drum that they all just gather around.'

He was aware that Big Jay had been speaking. He looked up. Big Jay was in tears.

'Hell's wrong?'

'It's Little Jay. She – she went to the bridge by the Drydock and tried to jump down onto the motorway. The police caught her, she's been sectioned for her own safety.'

Everyone looked stunned. Will kind of resented it. In his head he had been working on a routine about how the Chester portrayed in *Hollyoaks* was completely different from what the place was like and although he knew it would get a laugh another time by then he'd probably forget how it went.

If he hadn't been so busy with various things he might have been disturbed at how quiet everything had got. He spent most of his free time with Lorna, watching Fellini in the Elsix Picture House, touring the headshops in the Corn Exchange, eating out on Call Lane, walking in Hyde Park as the snow rotted in the grass. They developed little injokes and catchphrases and pressure points. It was getting serious; he felt like doing something for Valentine's Day. Weekend in the Lakes. The old man's cottage by Lake Windermere. Have to ask him soon. Everything else would be booked out.

When he wasn't with Lorna he was hitting the books. The PGCE was conditional on a two one. He didn't want to end up coasting now. This was final year. He was busy and his mates would be busy. Don't be like the Social regulars who get caned at free parties every weekend and Wikipedia their coursework. Time to grow up.

So he felt no disquiet at the lack of contact from his friends. The texts dropped off, even the texts from Gallo: normally the loquacious bastard pestered him daily. The odd time he got a look at Facebook, Lorna checking it with his Dell in bed in the mornings, he noticed his friend count seemed to be dropping, and there were fewer event invitations. He could be imagining it; he had 597 friends, and you'd maybe not miss a few. Could you maybe find out who had defriended you? Welcome to Stalkerville. Population: you.

On his way across to Kensington Terrace (keeping his head up and eyes over the shoulder as he passed the Asians in the street; there were loads of them now) he spotted Gallo, on the other side of Brudenell. It was only a two-lane road, and the guy had no iPod Will could see; still, when Will shouted him, he did not reply. Will puzzled over this for a moment or so and then it was forgotten.

He hit the Turkish supermarket for cheap food and arrived at Lorna's loaded down with bags. Lorna's mates from Headingley were there and he was introduced around.

'Hey. Didn't I see you at a party? Dressed as Lara Croft?'

The guy shook his head. 'No way. Imperialist propaganda. I mean, she breaks into ancient temples and steals religious relics. It should be banned.'

'I thought maybe you were dressing as her in an ironic way,' Will said.

Lorna said: 'Irony makes everything all right.'

Walking through to Lorna's corridor of a kitchen, unpacking meat, vegetables, pulses, dressing, and the vibrato of a text in his inside jacket. 'This is the real test of our relationship. Whether you can cook.'

'If I fail –'

' – we eat you. If you pass –'

'You'll still eat me, hopefully,' Will said, and that got a laugh.

They were just serving up when the knock came. Lorna went to get it. Underneath the talk of politics and exercise and other people Will heard sounds that should not be in his life. Low voices and radio sparks.

A man appeared in the dining room doorway. He wore a cheap suit. Hulking guys in fluorescent and body armour behind him. Conversation stopped.

'Are you Will Handsworth?'

'Yes.'

The ice was back in his chest. The guy said that he was DC Chad Stern from Burley Park CID. He said he wanted to talk to Will in connection with an incident that occurred during the early hours of January 9. If he could come to the station. Yes, it had to be now. Will walked through the space towards the cop and knew that he was walking the line from one world into the next, and in this next world there would be no PGCE, no Lego girl, no cottage in Lake Windermere. He slipped from one world into the next and it was a painless and creepy experience, like a BCG. His chest was packed and creaking with ice.

He followed DC Stern to the marked car and did not look around because if he saw anyone's face, anyone who knew him, then they would also have heard about him, and come to the worst conclusion in the base of their hearts. It was a sensation that affected him far more than the act and the crime ever would. He wanted to turn around and let them know that they had it all wrong, that it wasn't him doing this bad thing, that the bad thing wasn't bad when he did it, because he was not the kind of person who did this kind of thing! *Do you hear me! I am not the kind of person who does this kind of thing!*

Matthew Bellwood

An Icy Man

Imagine a village in the Yorkshire Dales; a little village nestled in a snow-covered valley. The lanes glitter with frost; the rooftops of the houses are fringed with tiny icicles; the cars shine silver in the moonlight.

The village is still and silent in the winter air; the people in it, for the most part, fast asleep. And as they sleep – they dream...

But not everyone here is sleeping now. On the outskirts of the village, the houses thin out until there is nothing but open fields and standing in one of these fields is an ancient farmhouse.

The door flies open. A red-haired woman stomps out into the frosty air. She marches across to an old fiesta, rusting in the yard.

'Alice!' A second woman appears in the doorway. 'Fuck off,' says the redhead.

She flings a black leather bag on to the passenger seat and crawls in after it, slamming the car door shut behind her.

'Alice,' the woman calls again.

The engine suddenly shudders into life and the twin beams of the headlights cut into the darkness, illuminating the lane that leads that off into the village. The second woman frantically starts pulling on her shoes. But she is too late.

The ancient car sets off into the night, its balding tyres slicing in half a young weasel that has been foolish enough to run into its path.

'Alice,' screams the woman at the door again. She runs out after the car into the frozen yard and slips on the remains of the eviscerated weasel, landing with a bang on the frost covered ground.

Time Passes. Not forwards but backwards. Another village. Another house.

A little girl sits by an open fire, wrapped in a thick, green towel. Her long, blonde hair is wet and clings to her head in fat, yellow, rats' tails. Beside her is a mug of warm milk and next to it, a tower of crumbly digestive biscuits. The girl ignores these things and stares intently at the man sitting opposite her.

'Where's mummy?' she asks.

Time passes again. It is two o'clock in the morning. Alice has been gone for nearly three hours and Laura has barely moved for the last two and a half. The fire is out and the door to the farmhouse hangs open. Outside, the snow is falling.

It has taken Laura twenty minutes to scrape the weasel from her shoe and another ten to wash her hands afterwards. Since then she has spent the evening drinking. She is lying now, slumped in an armchair in the living room, a glass of wine in her hands.

It does not surprise her that Alice has left. That has been in the air for some time. Tonight's argument was not really about anything – just a stupid excuse for Alice to go. Geoffrey, her old and incontinent cat had peed in Alice's bag again. Hardly grounds for a divorce. She rubs her belly with the flat of her hand. It doesn't surprise her. But it hurts though. Like someone has suddenly cut through her guts with a pair of tiny sewing scissors.

Geoffrey grizzles upon her lap and she scratches his ears affectionately. Fifteen years they have been together, she and Geoffrey. Longer than her marriage to Neil and this –

whatever it was – with Alice, put together.

'Just think,' mutters Laura. 'She wanted me to get rid of you. Poor puss! Poor puss! Couldn't do that, could I?'

Geoffrey yawns, his thin, pink tongue taut and straining in his mouth. Laura follows suit. She knocks back the rest of the wine in the glass and then reaches for the bottle of chardonnay she has hidden behind the chair. As she does, her eyes are caught by the patterns of the frost upon the window. Beautiful, she thinks; like frozen cobwebs. If she stares at it long enough, it is almost possible to make out shapes in the rime of frost: waterfalls and animals and even people.

Sipping her wine, she imagines the world that these frostbitten creatures might inhabit. Geoffrey purrs as she does so like a slightly malodorous hot-water bottle. She strokes him gently, enjoying the warmth of his presence in the lonely room. Her eyelids droop.

'Where's mummy?' the girl asks again.

'Sh – she's not here.'

The man looks embarrassed. He is a funny looking person – tall and skinny with wild hair that sticks out at odd angles. It makes him look like someone from a cartoon. That is why she went with him in the first place. She knows she ought to be careful with strangers. But the man had looked so strange that she had almost felt sorry for him.

'Where is she?'

'I – I don't know. I expect she's at your house.' 'Can I see her?'

The man looks away. 'I don't think so.'

'She'll be sad if I'm not there.'

'Yes, I know.'

'What are we going to do?'

'Well. I don't know. Maybe we should take some more pictures.'

'Alright,' the girl says. 'What shall we dress as this time?'

'I – I don't know,' says the stranger. 'Come on. L- let's have a look in the box.' He smiles and his strange, pale face seems to glow.

Laura opens her eyes. Her head is aching. She knocked it pretty hard when she slipped in the yard. She puts a hand to her brow and a tune seems to wander into her brain. She finds herself smiling. She started to teach Alice to dance to this tune – back when they had just moved in together. Back at the beginning of – well ... whatever. Never try teaching a redhead to tango. That's one little life lesson she won't forget. They danced every night for the first two months they spent in the house together. Arguing and treading on each other's toes and holding each other in the firelight. It had been wonderful. Mills and Boon romantic.

She takes another swig of wine and feels the swallow turn into a yawn. Perhaps a walk will do her good – help her clear her head. She lifts Geoffrey gently from her lap, jumps to her feet and stamps out into the hallway. She slings on the old and tatty duffle coat she wears for cleaning the chickens out and pulls on her Wellingtons. They're an old pair she has had since before she was married. Alice had doctored them for her as a Christmas present and they now each sport a tiny, red tongue and a pair of goggly, plastic eyes.

It has begun to snow quite thickly now. She can no longer see the stars any more. She steps outside and pulls the farmhouse door shut behind her.

'I'm tired,' says the little girl. 'Is it nearly bedtime?' 'Not yet,' says the man. She starts to cry.

'What's the matter?' he asks.

'I want mummy.'

The man sits down beside her. He puts a skinny arm

around her shoulder and pulls her close to him. He is skin and bones. The girl sobs into his pale blue shirt.

'I want her,' she says.

'I know,' says the man. 'I want my mummy sometimes.'

The girl stops crying and looks at him. 'Where's your mummy?'

'I don't know. She – she went away when I was little. I- I didn't know her very well.'

'That's sad,' says the girl.

'Yes,' says the man. 'But it doesn't matter. I've got you now.'

'Yes,' she says. She takes hold of one of his fingers. Her hands are tiny compared to his. His fingers are long and cold – like icicles.

Laura has walked for nearly a mile now, tramping across the frozen fields. She is starting to think that perhaps coming out was not a good idea. The wine she has drunk is making her feel sick and the bruise on her head is not helping.

'Bugger, bugger, bugger,' she chants, stamping her feet in a vain attempt to encourage the circulation. It's important to keep moving. People have frozen to death on nights like this. She takes a breath and trudges on through the snow. She cannot help but think of Alice. Memories come unbidden to her brain, and play themselves out in glorious technicolour.

She remembers a self-defence class in the parish hall. Thirteen ladies and 'give-it-to-me Gwynn' the local policeman.

Practicing an elbow jab, her hand encounters Alice's face. Blood spurts across the hall in an arc. Two people scream and Alice falls to the floor, clutching her nose. Laura stands and looks at the blood. The little droplets shine like rubies on the floorboards.

Everyone gathers themselves around Alice in a genteel scrum of sympathy. Give-it- to-me Gwynn pushes his way through. 'Stand back ladies, I'm going to administer emergency first aid.' As he speaks, Mrs Norse-Foreleg, the plus-size-lady from the Post Office, falls to the floor in a fit of blatant attention seeking. 'She's fainted!' someone cries. This is debatable. What is certain however is that she has landed on the willowy frame of Christine Roberts, from the Arts and Crafts shop, who has folded up like a human deckchair and is whimpering like an otter.

Attention shifts to this new source of excitement. As it does, Alice catches Laura's eye and together, they make a swift exit. It is whilst she is busy apologising to her friend in the warmth of Alice's Ford Fiesta that Alice leans forward and kisses her for the very first time.

'Bugger, bugger, bugger...' she chants again.

It seems unfair somehow that she should be forced to feel so bad about Alice's leaving. After all, it is her lack of commitment that has caused Alice to go in the first place. Her gutlessness, as she calls it – her unwillingness to admit to their relationship, to take part in public displays of affection, to proclaim her lesbianity loudly to the world.

Laura chews her lip in the falling snow. Alice's face seems to float before her, like a lantern, leading her on. Perhaps Alice is right. She has always been a gutless lover; unable to commit. There has always been some part of her terrified by the thought of it ... getting lost in someone else ... drowning in a relationship.

She stares down at her frozen feet. The goggly eyes of the doctored Wellington boots stare back up at her.

'Will you look after me?' the man asks. The two of them are sitting in the window of the house. It is snowing outside.

'Alright,' she says.

The man smiles. 'That's good.' He looks down at his feet

and then glances at her sideways.

'Can I kiss you?' he asks.

The little girl shrugs. 'Alright. If you want.'

The man's pale skin pinkens slightly. He picks her up with both hands and swings her round so that she is sitting on his lap. Then he pushes his face towards her. 'What are you doing?' she asks.

'Kissing you,' he says.

'That's not how you kiss someone.'

'It is sometimes.' he says. He leans forward and does it again. The little girl laughs. 'You're funny,' she says.

'You're funny too,' he tells her.

The little girl hugs him and pushes her cheek into his chest. The man strokes her hair with his long, cold fingers.

'Do it again,' she says. 'The kissing thing.' 'Alright,' says the man.

The affair had all been Alice's idea and she had jumped at it at first. It had seemed like a chance to prove that she could live without Neil; that life went on and that she would not be stranded or scuppered by his leaving.

A lesbian affair! It had seemed somehow daring at the time. Laura had felt like a new woman – capable of changing – able to become someone else at the drop of a hat, or the loss of a husband ...

She blinks as a snowflake scores a direct hit and melts onto her eyeball.

Not that she had any right to blame him. He had asked her many times to go with him. 'A new start in the New World'. She had even gone out there once to see the house that he had found for her. To see the office where he would work and the beach and the bars where they would chill in the sun and drink and talk and laugh. And there had been a moment on the beach in the dawn, when he had put out his arms and pulled her close to him that she had almost believed in it.

But something had stopped her. Some kind of wriggling fear had made its presence felt in the pit of her belly and told her that Australia was not the place for her. And so he had left; flown off to a new job and a new life in the sun. She had kissed him goodbye at the airport; smiled at him with red-rimmed eyes as he had left the departure lounge; cried as the plane had taken off into the grey and rainy sky; and almost written to him every day for the first six months that she had spent in Britain on her own. She had felt at the time as though he had taken a part of her away with him – as though he had stolen some semi-vital organ like a single lung or a kidney. And yet she had let him go. Had ignored his entreaties to go out and visit him ... had forgotten to send him a Christmas card last year. And with time, the feeling had faded.

Laura trudges on, kicking the snow out of her way and as she does, her foot slips suddenly, her ankle sliding down a frozen rabbit hole. Laura yelps and finds herself falling backwards into a drift of new-laid snow.

She lies there for a moment, feeling the world spin dizzyingly around her. There is something comforting about the cold. It would be easy to stay here ...

She sits up abruptly and shakes her head to clear it, knocking the snowflakes from her hair and trying to ignore the slightly sickly feeling in her belly.

It is at this moment that the figure steps out in front of her. She almost does not notice him at first, so perfectly is he camouflaged against the falling snow. And yet he is there. In the way that a person glimpsed in shadow can appear nothing more than a deeper black within the darkness, so the icy figure is somehow a deeper whiteness within the snow.

She freezes. The shape in the snow is motionless. It could be a statue – a piece of outdoor sculpture or something like that. But who would put a sculpture in a field behind a farmhouse? For a crazy moment, she thinks that perhaps it is Alice – come back to apologise and ask for her forgiveness. But Alice has never apologised for anything in her life. It is always Laura who does the apologising.

Laura stands. She and the stranger watch each other for a moment. Then the voice comes.

'Hello, Laura.' It is a strange voice: thin and fragile yet oddly beautiful, like the ringing sound a glass makes if you hit it with a spoon.

'Who are you? How do you know my name?'

'Laura,' says the voice again.

'I've got a knife with me, you know. I didn't come out here unprotected.'

Silence.

'What do you want, you ... you bastard? Come on, show yourself.'

The figure lurches suddenly towards her, tottering forwards on spindly legs. As it does, its true nature is suddenly revealed.

'Who the ... Oh my God, what are you?'

The thing before her looks down at its feet in what appears to be abject misery. Then it lifts its head and stares at Laura with a look of mournful longing in its eyes.

'I don't know,' it says.

The creature is one of the oddest things that she has ever seen. He appears to be made entirely out of snow and ice. His body is long and thin and spindly, like one of those aliens that Americans keep seeing. He looks so brittle, that Laura is sure that if she were to touch him, his fragile form would simply crumble in her hands.

His face is likewise small and delicate. A tiny mouth, a tiny nose and two black eyes that shine like polished coal. But in contrast to his thin and skeletal body, his face is surrounded by a shimmering silver mane: a wild explosion of punky, frozen hair – like an icy version of a tribal mask.

'I ... you ... I ...' it says.

Laura keeps her mouth closed. What does one say in situations like this? She racks her brains, trying to think of a suitable opening gambit. There isn't one. And so she decides that she'd better start off with the basics.

'Hi, I'm Laura.'

The creature flinches and peers at her arm. Laura hastily pulls it away. For a moment, she wonders what Alice would do. Kick him in the balls and then run away she thinks. But that doesn't seem to be an option. The creature seems more frightened of her than she is of him. And besides, although she has no proof of the matter, he does not seem to have any balls. Certainly he doesn't appear to be wearing any clothes.

Laura clears her throat and tries again. 'So ... Do you ... live locally?' 'I live here,' he says.

'What ... What do you mean? In the field?'

'No,' he says. 'In the snow...'

ROSA CAMPBELL

Antarctica

Tonight I saw a map of Antarctica.
The very tip of the world
in green and blue and bone,
quadrants and degrees,
typefaces.

The South Pole was barely a dot.
Ninety degrees South, latitude.
All lines of longitude converge
at both poles,
you know.

I am lying on my bed and I am
fifty-six degrees North, latitude
and two degrees West, longitude –
an approximation, but
thereabouts.

If I travelled just two point eight degrees
East of here, I would reach
the Prime Meridien, and
I could follow it down
to Antarctica.

I would start in the United Kingdom,
head for France, Spain and the Med,
before reaching Algeria, Mali,
Burkina Faso, Togo,
Ghana.

From there on out it's nothing but sea.
I would swim right through the Equator,
the Atlantic and Southern oceans,
to Queen Maud Land, claimed
by Norway.

And whilst I swim I will picture
the very tip of the world.
All lines of longitude converge
at both poles,
you know.

ROSA CAMPBELL

Melville

Sat surrounded by rented boxes
in your almost-empty room
with the little window open and
the cold smell of fresh rain and
your suitcases half-packed and
a couple of mismatched cider cans
the only things on the shelf, I wait
for you to get back with money so
we can pay the guys to take away
our books and put them in storage
for the summer months whilst
you go north and I go back t'North and
we both feel the effects of what you
(on the end of the pier last night)
termed 'apartness' and I don't know
if you meant to be poetic but my god,
there's nothing but poetry here.

SJ Bradley

The Life of Your Dreams

They were giving her everything she needed to build the rocket. Bolts, sheets, fusion conversion unit, fuel pipe, sparkers. All of it in the package, sliding down the ramp towards her. Sitting in the barn entrance, Anna watched a Ganglian worker push the box away from his little truck. It was long enough for half of it to land in shadow.

Beetles crawled around the doorway, segments of their long brown bodies glowing bronze in the sun. Anna watched them as the worker turned. Silently he got back into his truck, and drove away without a word. That would be the last Anna saw of the Ganglians for twelve days.

Anna tore open the lid. A sheet taped inside read: 'Anna 51628: To be returned if incomplete 96.84, and worker 51628 to return to usual duties.' The glare of the sun landed hard on Anna's shaved head, and she glanced up at the greenhouses. The sound of the hydration sprays pulsed through the polycarbonate sheeting. At the near end she could make out two shapes: men, standing side by side, their hands in the rhyberry branches. They would be picking the green-gold fruit, and laying them into the punnets. The Ganglians didn't like their berries crushed. Even a single bruised fruit meant a whole box discarded. The work quota was eight perfect punnets a day. Work over quota, and you could earn an extra stamp on your clock card. Twenty stamps for a bottle of vodka the size of a bottle of nail polish. Forty for a sanctioned hour off work. Five hundred for a rocket.

Inside, lifeless dials mounted on a board met a curved tube like an exhaust. Hearing a sound in the corner, Anna turned. A man wearing goggles had his metal sheeting welded together in a long hexagon. The pieces made a narrow column too thin, too close, for an adult's shoulder. Wiping his brow, the man pushed his mask back. 'Hello there,' he called. 'You here building your rocket pack?'

Anna allowed the components to fall back into the box. They landed with a soft clatter. 'There aren't any instructions,' she said. 'I don't know where to start.'

'Come down,' he said kindly. 'Have a look at mine.'

His corduroy trousers were scorched, burned flat with sparks form the work. Between his feet stood a small engine. What looked like a thick rubber band held one cog to another. The whole mechanism together was no larger than a driver for a toy train. 'Is this it?' she said.

Talk in the sleep tins said a rocket could get you home. Back to Earth, with its high waters and scorched ground. It was a place Anna had once been desperate to escape. Live the life of your dreams on Ganglian-A, the advertisements had promised, and Anna had believed it. She and a friend, Urtka, had scrabbled the money together to pay the passage to get here. Anna had got hers hustling pool. Urtka, staying out late in the evenings, had brought home a twenty here, a twenty there. Anna hadn't wanted to ask how she'd come by it.

The carrier they'd come in was a vessel shaped like a tumble drier drum. Anna had ridden with somebody's feet in her nose, and somebody else's child under her armpit. The air had been too stuffy to waste it talking. Feeling the metal tremble through the mass of bodies, Anna had been able to make out the top corner of Urtka's ear, squeezed next to a beard and an elbow. Coming past Mars, past Saturn, or so Anna imagined, Anna felt the sides grow cold, and tried to count the Earth days. If there was a toilet none of them ever found it. She rounded Pluto with somebody's urine dripping down her cheek. It is close now, she told herself. It is close. She thought it worthwhile for what awaited them at the other end.

Weeks later, a corner of the ship hit solid ground. The bottom end opened, and bodies shaken out by some power above. Falling, Anna saw arms, legs, frozen to the sides of the can, torn loose from their owners. She landed on a pile of the dead. Scrambling free, she'd seen Ganglians in work uniforms shovelling corpses into a pit by the landing pad. It looked dug for the purpose. Anna climbed to the top, and saw Urtka's lifeless form tumbling into the hole. Work started on the second day.

Tinkering, the man said: 'I was an engineer, on Earth. And sometimes little things can pack a punch. They're more powerful than you'd think, to look at them.' Up close his rocket looked even more like a child's toy.

'This doesn't look big enough for a dog,' she said.

The man smiled sadly. 'You catch on fast,' he said. 'Most people don't realise until they've put their own together. They hope it'll seem different out of the box.' Leaning back, he went on: 'Twelve days off work isn't to be sniffed at, though.' There was a mark around his eyes, a red rim left by the goggles. 'I come here as often as I can afford to. It's the best reward you can buy, I think.'

Still standing, Anna looked at the tools mounted on the wall. A hammer and wrench hung on hooks beside a screwdriver and a rope. 'Well,' she said, 'That's not enough for me.'

Taking an adjustable spanner from the rack, she looked through a crack in the wall at the greenhouses. She could see the spray from the irrigation system splashing on the insides of the glass. Out in the heat, the bolts gleamed silver. Lashing the sheeting to the frame, they held the roof and walls steady. Anna looked down at her own hands, dry and cracked from working all day in the wet. She imagined loosening the bolts; seeing the greenhouse lid slide loose, and the copper glare of the nearest star shining on the workers' skin as the walls and roof fell down. Down in the corner of the barn, the man hammered tacks into their homes in his project. Anna slid an adjustable torque-wrench into her pocket. 'I'm going to work outside,' she said.

DAN ANNETT was originally from Tyrella, Northern Ireland, He has just completed his first year of undergraduate study at the the University of Leeds, where he reads English Literature & History of Art. He was a Commended Foyle Young Poet during 2011 and has recently curated his first exhibition, *Out of the Shadows*, for Enjoy Art Space, Leeds. Daniel regards his poems as the outcome(s) of the opening/closing, breaking/making, fixing/blurring of thought ex nihilo. They are the process of constant inconsistency. (Blog: voicevoid.tumblr.com)

CRISTINA ARCHETTI follows her questions wherever they might lead. She is a guerrilla researcher, a qualified boxing instructor, a failed knitter, and accidental creative writer. The University of Salford, her employer, thinks she is a Senior Lecturer in Politics & Media. She is interested in terrorism, war, the impact of communication technologies on politics and society, journalism. Currently, she is plotting the overthrow of the higher education publishing industry by using stories to disseminate academic research. (Twitter: @Cristina_a)

JENNY BEECH was born on Easter Saturday, 1993, and wants to be a writer. She works as a nanny in Leeds. (Blog: theforceofwilber.wordpress.com)

MATTHEW BELLWOOD is a writer and storyteller based in Leeds. Over the last few years, he has worked everywhere from the Canadian Fringe to the International Shakespeare Conference in New Zealand. Along the way, he has performed in schools, libraries, theatres and pop-up museums, at DIY rock gigs and, on one memorable occasion, to an audience of 1,200 girl-guides in a tent. His stories range in style from traditional myths and folktales to interpretations of well-known literary classics. He also performs his own material – mainly stories about his life growing-up in Leeds.

SJ BRADLEY's work has appeared in various journals and anthologies, including Untitled Books. In 2013 she was shortlisted for the Willesden Herald International Short Story prize. She is one of the organising parties behind Leeds-based DIY literary social Fictions of Every Kind. She lives with her partner and cat. (Blog: sjbradleybooks.blogspot.com)

SARAH BROOKS spent several years teaching English in China, Japan and Italy, and is currently finishing a PhD in classical Chinese ghost stories at the University of Leeds. She is a member of the Leeds Writers' Circle and attended the Clarion West Writers' Workshop in summer 2012. Her poems have been published in *Mslexia*, and a story is forthcoming in Shimmer Magazine.

JOSHUA BYWORTH was born in Northampton in 1991 and grew up in Phnom Penh and Oxford. He is soon to graduate from University of Leeds where he has read English Language and Literature, and although plans for the future are predictably thin on the ground he would like to continue writing in any way that he can. Aside from a few student collections this is his first piece to be published.

ROSA CAMPBELL is twenty-two years old and frequently gets the panicked feeling that she should have a bit done more with her life by now. She was born and bred in Leeds, and is currently studying for her undergraduate degree in English Literature at the University of St Andrews, where she will next year be writing her dissertation on contemporary poetry under the supervision of Professor Don Paterson. Rosa's poetry has been published in her university literary journal, and she is currently President of

Inklight, the Creative Writing Society at St Andrews. She is also a full-time feminist and part-time travel addict. She blogs about books at rosareads.tumblr.com, and can be found on Twitter at @rosaetc.

MAX DUNBAR was born in London in 1981. He has recently finished a full-length novel, and his short fiction has appeared in various print and web journals. He also writes criticism for *3:AM* and *Butterflies and Wheels*. He blogs at maxdunbar.wordpress.com and tweets at @MaxDunbar1.

GARETH DURASOW has quite a lot to do with Leeds. It has educated, nurtured, distracted and hospitalised him. Leeds has made an indelible impact upon Gareth insofar as he doesn't remember much about particular evenings/mornings spent here. The last few times his work was published, it appeared in magazines such as *Angel Exhaust*, *Cadaverine*, *Polluto*, *The Rialto* and *Shearsman*. This was a year ago, or thereabouts. He teaches in Leeds.

AISSA GALLIE works as a business development manager and recently started her own business as a communication and personal development consultant. The LS13 competition marks her first step out of the closet to fulfill her lifelong ambition as a writer. Originally from Brixton, Aissa, age 36, has lived in Leeds off and on since the age of 5 and is now settled in Meanwood with husband Ritchie and two sons, Bernie and Bruce.

LIZZI HAWKINS is a young writer living and studying in Leeds, Yorkshire. She writes predominantly poetry and draws heavily on the contrast of her city/country surroundings. She writes and performs with the Ilkley Young Writers group, and has recently read as part of the Ilkley Literature Fringe Festival.

AJ KIRBY is the award-winning author of five published novels, two collections of short stories, three novellas and over fifty published short stories, which can be found widely in print anthologies, magazines and journals and across the web. His second novel *Paint this Town Red* was shortlisted for the Guardian's Not the Booker Prize 2012, and his short fiction has won numerous awards at UK literary festivals. He is also a sportswriter for the Professional Footballers' Association, and his full-length book about football is slated for publication in Spring 2013. Finally, he's a fiction reviewer for *The Short Review* and *The New York Journal of Books*.

ADAM LOWE is a writer, publisher and producer from Leeds. In 2009 he received four Lambda Award nominations and three British Fantasy Award nominations. In 2008, his magazine, *Polluto*, was awarded the Spectrum Fantastic Art Silver Editorial Award. In 2011, he was a finalist for the Eric Hoffer Award in Best New Writing. A guerilla literature activist, he believes in bringing literature to unusual spaces.

ZODWA NYONI is a Zimbabwean-born performance poet, playwright and workshop facilitator. She started writing with Leeds Young Authors (LYA), a community-based performance poetry group in 2005. As a member of LYA, she represented the United Kingdom at the Brave New Voices International Youth Poetry Slam in New York City, USA in 2006. She has also led poetry workshops in schools, prisons and community groups in Yorkshire and Lancashire. She has worked as a Guest Website Editor for the Arts Council Yorkshire's Decibel Young Leaders initiative. The initiative worked to support and raise the profile of artists of African, Asian and Caribbean descent in England.